Ten Was The Deal:

Southern Hunting And Fishing Stories

By

John P. Faris, Jr.

Illustrations By
Ralph Mark

First published by Dog Ear Publishing
4010 W. 86th Street, Ste H
Indianapolis, IN 46268
www.dogearpublishing.net

ISBN: 978-1-4575-2100-3

This book is printed on acid-free paper.

Some of the anecdotal accounts in this book are true. Others are composites of factual situations. However, certain liberties have been taken in the interest of creating a compelling narrative. In many cases names, characters, businesses, organizations, places, events, and incidents have been altered to protect the identity of real individuals. In those instances, any resemblance to any person, living or dead, events, or locales is entirely coincidental.

Printed in the United States of America

This is an Our Home Place, Inc. book.

John P. Faris, Jr. also contributed a story
to *Outdoor Adventures in the Upcountry*, Hub City Press,
Spartanburg, South Carolina 2010.

... choose you this day whom ye will serve; ...but as for me and my house, we will serve the Lord.

Joshua 24:15
King James Version

Contents

Dedication

This book is dedicated first to my mom and dad. Dad taught me, at a very early age, to love and respect the outdoors. He kindled in me a passion for hunting and fishing. My mom accompanied us on many outings. She dropped me at countless farm ponds and duck hunting creeks when Dad had to work.

Also, to Claudia, my wife of forty-five years, who happily joins me on many trips to strange places. She has generously allowed me the time to put some of my experiences to paper.

To our daughter, Ashley, and our son, John, for being the motivation for many an adventure. They gave me immeasurable joy while I was teaching them what I had learned about God's great creation.

And last, to our five grandchildren, Cameron, Kaleb, Joshua, Grace, and Bailey. I pray that God will give me time to show them the red hills, hardwood river bottoms, and salt marshes of my beloved southern outdoors.

To The Reader

Christmastime at our house has always been a very big season of family gatherings and gift giving.

Once my two children, Ashley and John, grew up and had families of their own, picking out Christmas presents for them became much harder. In 2006, I decided that instead of buying something, I would write each a story.

I had never written anything in my life, but I have a very close friend, a pastor, who writes a story every Christmas and reads it on Christmas Sunday to his congregation. On many occasions my wife and I received a copy of these special stories as a Christmas present. I was so inspired, I wrote John and Ashley each an original story for Christmas 2006.

I had a good time writing these two outdoor stories. The children were surprised, and they seemed to sincerely like what I had written, so I was pleased.

I did not write another story until my dad's ninety-first birthday. It took a lot of time, but it seemed to bring joy to my dad. I felt a very real sense of satisfaction. This was the first time the idea of actually writing enough stories to make a book entered my mind.

In May of 2011 my dad, then ninety-five, became critically ill following a stroke. The days before he died he was very weak. He could not open his eyes or speak.

At that time I wrote about the last hunting trip we had taken together. I picked a time when he was alone; no other family members, no nurses. I carried those tearstained pages to his bedside, and I managed with breaking voice and blurred eyes, to read the story to him. My dad never moved. I wasn't even sure he had heard me. As I rose to go, I took his hand. Big tears ran down his cheeks. He had heard every word, and we had said our final goodbye.

Dad died the next day.

It was then I was sure I would write this book.

As you read it, you will know I have had a wonderful life filled with many outdoor adventures, so often made more enjoyable because they were spent with my dad.

Introduction:

FISHING WITH MY DAD

I like to fish. I like to fish a lot. The first time I can recall going fishing was in 1949. I was four years old.

My Dad, who was thirty-four that year, had been back home from the Navy four years. Dad and I were best buddies by this time, and we remained so until his death sixty-one years later.

Mom tells the story of my dad returning from Japan in 1945. I was eight months old. I had been born while he was at sea. When Dad returned from the war, he was so excited to see me, his firstborn baby, but I would have absolutely nothing to do with this stranger. I had never seen him before! I must have gotten over it pretty quickly, because Dad was my best friend from my earliest memory.

Dad kept an old wooden boat chained to a big red oak tree at Blazer's, a fish camp right where the bridge crossed Greenwood Lake. The gradual, sloping shore was sand and small gravel. It was not hard to pull the boat up and secure it, and a good number of fishermen stored their boats there.

There was a small monthly charge paid to the fish camp owners who kept an eye on the boats and offered fuel, bait, ice, and other general supplies. This day we would only need a gallon of gas and some engine oil. The bait we would use my dad had caught himself.

After loading the small Johnson outboard motor, tin minnow bucket, glass minnow trap, and metal cooler into the trunk of the family Plymouth, we started out to my grandfather's farm. That's where Dad caught the minnows and maintained his unique live well.

My grandfather's farm was about five miles from town, off the Princeton Road. I really enjoyed this part of the fishing trip a great deal. There was a beautiful, bold creek that ran through long, wide, grassy bottoms on my grandparents' small cattle farm. It was hard for me to imagine, but years later Granddaddy would tell me that when he bought the farm, that bottomland had been covered with big trees. He wanted to turn this valley into a pasture for raising whiteface Hereford cows, so in the 1930s he decided to have the land cleared of trees.

He told me how Mr. Warren Tinsley, a neighbor farmer who many years later became my father-in-law, hired a crew of men to clear the bottoms. As I mentioned, the farm was located about five miles from town. Granddaddy told me that the men would bring their axes with them, walk from town, and be ready to go to work at first light. They were paid fifty cents an hour. It took the better part of a year to cut the trees, grub out the stumps, and burn the slash. Now, it was a beautiful, fertile pasture with thick grass inhabited by very healthy, fat, young calves with their moms.

When Dad and I arrived, he unloaded the minnow bucket which he let me carry, and he brought the glass minnow trap. He held my hand as we opened and closed the big wooden gate. We headed down the gradual slope and across the pasture to the creek.

For the live well Dad had built a wooden frame and covered it with hardware cloth with quarter-inch square holes. This wire box, complete with hinged lid, fit snuggly in between the steep banks of the little creek. The two-inch minnows he caught were let out into this box where they stayed in the fast-flowing, clear, cool creek until time to go fishing.

When we first got there, Dad filled the minnow bucket with creek water and just let it sit awhile. He let me put the bait into the glass minnow trap and screw on the galvanized top. Then we lowered the trap into a nice, deep pool in the stream. By now the minnow bucket was cool. Dad poured out the water, filled it with fresh water, and let me dip out three dozen lively minnows from the minnow box. I really liked chasing the minnows around the box with the small net. As I caught them, I flipped them into the minnow bucket. When we returned later in the evening, we would put whatever minnows we had not used back into the box, take the newly caught ones from the trap, and put them in the box with the rest. We always had a good supply of fresh bait when we headed to Greenwood Lake.

As we started back to the car, Dad swapped and took the minnow bucket, now heavy with the water and minnows, and I got to carry the lighter glass minnow trap, very carefully.

We put a little bit of ice from the cooler into the minnow bucket, closed the trunk, and I climbed into the front seat and into my special chair. Dad had made it, and I sat in it when I was in the boat. It also fit into the front seat of the car.

This unique chair had started out as a child-size, cane-bottom, rocking chair. Dad had removed the rockers and attached flat, thin boards to the legs where the rockers had been. He put angled blocks on the back ends of these two boards.

He placed the chair in the front seat of the car and pushed it toward the back of the seat. The angle blocks would slip between the seat bottom and its back. The chair then sort of snapped into place and stayed put. Dad would settle me in, and I was able to sit up high and see out very well. When we got to the lake, Dad got the little chair out and moved it to the middle of the boat where it fit perfectly and kept me from being too close to the sides of the boat.

I believe I had the first child's car seat ever invented.

With me situated safely in the middle of the boat, Dad attached the Johnson outboard, filled the gas tank to the proper level with the gas and oil mixture, unlocked the chain, and slid the boat into the water where it rested with just enough of the bottom on the sandy shore to hold it there.

After loading the two rods and the cooler, Dad tied the little minnow bucket by its handle to the gunwale and eased the minnows into the lake water. When we were ready to put the minnows on our hook, they were acclimated to the water's temperature.

Dad put a small, orange life jacket on me and topped me off with a straw hat, a promise he made to Mom as a condition of our going. That done, he shoved the boat out into deeper water where he started the motor. A couple of pulls on the starter rope with an interim adjustment to the choke did the trick.

We were off to a quiet cove. We would not see another boat the whole afternoon.

In those early years, there were but a handful of summer cabins on Greenwood Lake. Now, sixty-five years later in 2012, there are few lots remaining for sale. Countless very expensive, year-round, residential, permanent, and vacation homes solidly line the shore.

When I was in high school, a classmate's father owned the Western Auto store in town. Among the other items he sold, there were black-and-white television sets. The story goes that one day a man came in to this store and traded a three-acre lakefront lot for a television. Today, that lot, which has a beautiful view, would sell for more than one-hundred-thousand dollars. But those things did not impress me back then. What did was that my dad was taking me fishing. It was a beautiful spring day, and I was spending all of it with my best friend.

We pulled into a quiet cove and dropped anchor near a shady, rocky outcrop.

Dad had a short steel rod for me rigged with a small Pflueger reel. It had a cork spool and pearl-colored handles. It had Supreme etched into one side. He got this ready with a long, sharp hook, a small split shot sinker, and a yellow cork with a bright red plug in the top. He adjusted the depth of the cork, pushed the red plug in good and tight, and hooked a spunky minnow right under its dorsal fin.

Lightly thumbing the reel's spool, Dad plopped the minnow five feet in front of the rocky outcrop. He handed me the rod and showed me what to do when I got a bite.

He again pulled in the minnow bucket, took the small net, caught another nice minnow, and proceeded to bait his own hook. All the while he was watching my cork and telling me what to do.

I was fascinated by the strong, frisky minnow pulling the cork this way and that. The cork bobbed and danced across the mirrored surface of the cove as the minnow swam three feet below the small, yellow sphere.

When the minnow swung to the outer limit of the line, Dad showed me how the minnow would climb to the surface in an unnatural way that required me to reel in the line so Dad could recast the bait. I liked reeling in the line. I liked it so well, I started doing this as soon as Dad had cast it out. He would patiently reposition the minnow, and, for the umpteenth time, tell me to leave it in the water or else a fish could never find it.

I finally listened to his advice long enough for beginner's luck to kick in.

The minnow swimming close to the rock ledge attracted the attention of a healthy, hungry bass.

Dad had already explained what to watch for. The action of the minnow telegraphed up to the cork would tell the story of what the fish was doing and what the minnow was seeing.

Just as he had said, the minnow, seeing the much bigger fish approach, became terrified. The cork that had been merrily bobbing along the surface before, now was frantically racing first this way, then that.

The quick jerky movements of the float sparked an immediate but involuntary jerk on the rod.

But Dad had caught the new action in his peripheral vision also and quickly said, "Don't pull yet. Let him run."

Within seconds, the minnow's erratic actions settled down into a steady and desperate course away from the dark water of the rock ledge.

Dad said, "See the fish is moving in on the minnow now. The minnow is swimming away, and the fish is chasing him. In a second, the fish will strip the scale from the minnow and then swallow him. Be ready. Wait until that happens before reeling in. I'll tell you when. Be ready. Be ready. Now!"

I began as fast as my little hands could go. As I took the slack out of the line, the cork shot below the surface, the line tightened, and my rod tip bent sharply.

I held on tightly and tried to reel. I was so excited I started turning the handle backward.

Dad noticed my mistake and quickly said, "Turn the handle the other way."

I reversed course and got the line tight again which caused the fish to race to the surface. I could see the line streaking through the water, unzipping the spring sky's blue reflection. The little one-pound largemouth bass shot into the air, cleared the surface by ten inches, turned a somersault, and splashed down.

After two more short runs and with Dad's gentle instructions, I led the fish over close enough for Dad to grab the line and pick the little fish up and over into the boat.

"Good job, Sonny Bo! Nice fish. Your very first fish!" Dad said.

"Can we take him home to show Mom?" I asked.

"Sure thing!" Dad replied with a big smile that matched my own.

An old black-and-white photograph taken in the living room of our small house reveals that my prize made it home for Mom's approval. There would be many, many more and bigger fish caught in the years to come, but the spring day in 1949 when I caught that little bass, is happily etched in my mind as one of the grandest days I ever spent fishing with my dad.

Best Dang Lard Ever Made

I jumped up onto the second slat from the bottom of the big, sagging wooden gate. In the glare of the 1949 Willys Jeep headlights, I lifted the heavy, rusted chain over the corner post.

It was pitch-black dark and twenty-five degrees. The chain froze to my fingers for a few seconds until the radiating warmth from my hands set them free. The crooked-hanging gate began to swing downhill. I held on and rode it open until it gradually ran aground in the frozen, spewed-up red clay.

The Jeep eased through. I closed the gate and with some effort looped the chain back over the old cedar post. As I climbed into the backseat next to Dad, I could see the old lady standing a short distance away. She was backlit by the oak fire under a #85 three-legged iron kettle. Hogs of several sizes were following her around, noisily announcing it was time for their breakfast.

Even in this freezing weather, she was wearing only her customary ankle-length, coarse cotton dress and bonnet. It completely shaded her face which I had never fully seen. Her name was Aunt Addie, at least that's what the four men in the Jeep called her. Aunt Addie was, as usual, stirring the contents of the big pot with a five-foot-long, thin, handcarved hickory paddle.

The Jeep eased through the side yard. The sandy surface had been swept clean with a brush broom. The headlights led us into the hardwoods. Looking over my shoulder, I could just make out the small .22 caliber pump rifle propped against the rickety backsteps of the two-story, unpainted clapboard farmhouse.

I knew from past trips like this what was going to happen next. As soon as we disappeared down the steep, rock hard, frozen red clay road toward the lake, we heard the sharp crack of the rifle.

"Dad, what's Aunt Addie shooting at this time of morning in the dark?" I asked.

The smooth hum of the four-wheel drive transmission was all the answer I got for a long minute. Then Dad said, "Well, ah, ah, she's just letting her family know it's soon time for breakfast."

I thought, *Wouldn't it be something if Mom called us to breakfast that way?*

Instead I said, "Oh! Is she cooking breakfast in that pot?"

"No," Dad said. "Aunt Addie raises hogs. She makes lard and sells it around the town square on Saturdays. She's rendering the lard in that big pot. She helps support her family that way."

Inside the Willys it was too warm. The five of us were crammed in, and I had on too many clothes not to be outside. We were easing down the narrow road toward the absolute best duck hunting hole in Laurens County. It was a real hot spot in the early 1950s. No outsider was ever invited to hunt on the Eubanks' farm. Its location was a closely guarded secret.

From my very first trip here I was warned never to mention that I had been hunting at Aunt Addie's place. I really did not understand exactly why, but the mystery of it all lent a heightened sense of excitement to a young boy's adventures.

The harsh headlights were piercing a tunnel into the darkness. The heavy hoarfrost had pushed up the red clay of the roadside banks a good three inches, and the crimson-tinted crystals sparkled and danced in the beams.

We crept on in low gear, trying not to hit the brakes, which might lock the wheels and cause us to slide out of control on the slick, frozen road. Down, down, down we drove, to the backwater of the big lake.

Lake Greenwood had been built in 1935 by constructing a dam across the Saluda River and Reedy River at a very narrow spot called Buzzards' Roost. The lake had 212 miles of shoreline. The damming of these two rivers flooded some of the most remote, least populated, and roughest country you ever saw. Todd's Quarter, where we were headed this freezing cold morning, was at the very heart of the area.

The four men I had been invited to hunt with today had been fast friends since my dad had returned to Laurens County after World War II. They hunted together almost every Saturday during the season, and for two years now I was usually with them.

It was a few days after Christmas. I would be eight years old in a few days and I had received from Santa Claus a Savage Arms .410-gauge shotgun. It was my first gun, not counting my much used Daisy pump BB gun. The single shot had a .22 caliber rifle barrel over the .410 barrel. Its single hammer was hard as heck for me to cock. It was the most wonderful gun in the world! Today I was equipped with my new gun, a pocket full of three-inch No. 6 shells, and a small, sharp L.L. Bean hatchet in a leather cover. I needed to be prepared for anything when I went into the big woods, I reasoned.

To miss one of these Saturday trips with my dad and his buddies would have been just about the worst thing I could imagine.

So no matter how cold or wet the weather, I was ready for the great adventures each of these trips promised.

Today would top the list.

Over the years I learned that Aunt Addie was a hard-working woman who was remotely kin to one of my dad's hunting pals. She was a churchgoing lady who had a no-good husband, a Eubanks. Aunt Addie's three sorry, unmarried sons lived with her: Percy, Wilbur, and Clint Eubanks.

It was said of these three boys that if you ordered a boxcarload of sorry and only got the Eubanks boys, you would have gotten your money's worth.

Aunt Addie ran a small herd of razorback hogs in the canebreak along the flooded backwaters of the Reedy River. She was known countywide for producing some of the best homemade sausage and lard, two staples of good southern cooking.

Her three sons, instead of working, ran moonshine whiskey. The reputation and demand for the Eubanks' white lightning was a testimony to their old family recipe and their attention to quality. The successful distribution of their illegal hooch was due more to an understanding of mutual coexistence with local law enforcement than to their marketing skills.

Game wardens and the county sheriff's deputies seldom entered Todd's Quarter. Folks that were overly zealous about enforcing the laws in this part of the county could expect an abbreviated life expectancy. However, the occasional obligatory raid by Alcohol, Tobacco, and Firearms (ATF) agents usually kept one of the Eubanks menfolk in the Atlanta penitentiary. Aunt Addie's husband was there now, serving his fifteenth month of a two-year sentence. These short Atlanta vacations from running shine were accepted within the family as part of their business model.

The unlawful sale of their quart jars of high-proof grain alcohol was never openly discussed around town, but apparently it was widely known among the male population of the county. As a matter of fact, by the time I was fourteen, and I don't remember anyone in particular telling me this, I was completely aware that one of the main points of availability was in the basement of a barbershop which sat not sixty yards from an active Pentecostal church.

The restroom, located in the basement of the barbershop, afforded a convenient excuse for many a patron to take a little nip of their recent purchase. The long lines for a haircut and shave at this establishment was the much-used excuse by many a husband who showed up late for Friday night supper.

The corn mash, an unwanted by-product of the liquor-making process, normally presented a problem of disposal. The Eubanks, however, had the perfect situation. They regularly dumped the mash in a creek that fed into the flooded timber of the lake. It so happens, this was an irresistible attractant for mallard ducks.

This steady source of free feed for the ducks and the remote location made Aunt Addie's farm tops in our book. The reputation of the Eubanks menfolk to fight at the drop of a hat was added assurance to Dad and his friends that neither game wardens nor any other hunters would be messing with us.

Not long after returning from the war, their friendships reestablished, Dad and his buddies soon realized the potential of the Todd's Quarter setup. The foursome went about making their duck hunting blind on the Eubanks farm. It was almost undetectable, but accessible any time of day. We could crawl into and out of this blind, and the ducks that were sitting on the water right in front of us wouldn't even know we were there. This was made possible by a narrow path that led from a large, deep gully up in the woods right into the back of the well concealed blind.

Years earlier, the four men had dug up knee-high young pines and cedars and planted them tightly together on both sides of the narrow path leading from the gully in the woods, all the way into the blind. Once these young trees got to growing, they were kept pruned. Before too long they made a fifty-yard-long evergreen tunnel that we could sneak down. There was no problem getting into the blind before daybreak, but should the group decide to go in the afternoon and there were already ducks on the water, we just parked way back up in the timber and eased down undetected.

They made the blind as permanent as these things get, and they made it roomy enough for half-a-dozen hunters at a time. That is to say, it was big enough for Sammy and me to tag along. Sammy was the grandson of one of Dad's hunting buddies and my younger boyhood hunting companion for many years.

There was another unique feature of this duck hunting spot. As you traveled up the winding tar-and-gravel road above the Eubanks' farm, there were several switchbacks, one of which lined up perfectly with the slough far below. If you pulled off and walked into the woods a short distance, you came out on a rocky ledge. Standing there gave you a high but direct view of the duck blind, and more importantly, any ducks sitting on the water nearby.

It was necessary to use very good binoculars to see at that distance, for without them it just looked like a lot of exposed stumps in the shallow backwater of the lake, a common sight. Dad kept an excellent pair of binoculars in the car all the time. They were a gift from the Captain of the aircraft carrier USS

Bennington, when Dad, the ship's gunnery officer, left the Navy in early 1946.

On our drives out into the country, Dad stopped at this curve. He and I would slip through the woods to this protected outcrop. He let me look through his binoculars. He put the strap around my neck and taught me how to focus them. We always compared the number of ducks the two of us counted. Many times there were so many we could not count them all. It was then we speculated the still must be running hard, and lots of mash was being dumped into the feeder creek near the duck blind.

Even with the binoculars and Dad directing my search, I could never pick out the duck blind itself. It was too perfectly blended into the surrounding vegetation.

There was one question that none of the cofounders of this little hunting mecca ever discussed in my presence or apparently tried to solve. It was, where was the exact location of the liquor still? No one in the group really wanted to know. The fountain-head of a nearly endless supply of duck-drawing manna remained a mystery.

The Jeep ground to a stop. The lights were cut off. We sat in total darkness for a few minutes until our eyes adjusted to the dark. Then we eased the Jeep down the road the last hundred yards and parked.

We all piled out of the new hunting vehicle, new to us that is. The Willys Jeep was ten years old. It had been acquired by a successful bid at a state-used equipment auction last summer. All of Dad's hunting buddies had chipped in to buy it, and it had proved a godsend.

Prior to acquiring this Jeep, we had used an older two-wheel drive truck. Frequently we had to push it when the slick red clay backroads of Laurens County threw us into a ditch. Even now, with the new vehicle, we still carried a sharp axe, two sturdy shovels, and a stout logging chain. Since the four-wheel drive purchase, however, we had not once been stuck while using this gift from above. If the temperature rose above freezing before we headed home this morning, it would prove a conclusive test. Climbing back up the steep road we had just descended, once thawed, would provide the ultimate challenge.

I was glad to get out. I was so excited, and I needed to pee. Apparently the anticipation, hot coffee, and a forty-minute drive affected more than just me. There was a lot of steam rising from the frozen ground around me.

From the dark, someone whispered, "Old dog never passes up an opportunity."

That necessary piece of business attended to, I slipped a half-dozen No. 6 .410-gauge shells in my right-hand jacket pocket, and broke open the little over/under Savage to be sure that it was unloaded. For two years now, since I had been allowed to go hunting with them, safety first was drilled into me by my dad and his friends. Now a week after Christmas, I had my first shotgun from Santa, and I desperately wanted to impress all of them with how grown-up I could be with this new responsibility. I closed the empty little over/under with a solid click.

Each man carried his shotgun, shells, and a croker sack of half a dozen or so crude hand-carved wooden decoys. I had my .410, a hatchet, and the thermos jug. Dad seemed to really like coffee after he came home from the Navy. In cold weather we did not travel far without steaming hot, black coffee.

We played silent follow the leader down the dark gully. Frightening images created by moonbeam shadows danced over the broken ground. Thank goodness I was fourth in line with Dad close behind.

I do not know what it was like for the adult men, but at my height, getting to the water's edge was like traveling through an evergreen tunnel. The planted pines and cedars grew thick on both sides and the boughs almost touched my shoulders as we slipped silently down into the roomy duck blind. When we got to the entrance, a whisper from the dark suggested that Dad put me in first with him next. Dad told me to go all the way to the far end of the blind. It was my favorite spot. There was no one to my left and Dad would be close beside me on my right. The other three men began unloading the decoys and taking them into the water. I stood up on the wide two-by-twelve bench and I could make out the men breaking the skim ice that extended twenty feet from the bank.

The decoys were being placed in an order which did not make sense to me at that point in my hunting experience. It must have been important because when they got done and waded through the very shallow water to shore, another two trips back out to rearrange one or two were necessary before everybody was satisfied.

As we all got situated in the blind, I heard the usual sounds of the last-minute clicking of shells being stuffed into the guns, spitting, throat clearing, and muffled coughs before silence descended.

It was cracking daylight in the eastern sky. Dad pulled up the left-hand sleeve of his heavy wool coat to check the time. On this cold, clear dawn, the ducks would come at fifteen minutes to seven. Even I had been enough times to a duck blind to know you could almost set your watch by it. The ducks were very punctual for their breakfast.

Dad said, "Go ahead and load up. Don't cock the hammer, though, until I tell you."

The oldest member of the group said softly, "Let Johnny take the first shot."

Whether it was the cold or just the excitement, I was shivering pretty good. The sun would rise behind us, keeping our faces in the shadows and the incoming ducks silhouetted in the morning's cloudless sky.

Even so, Dad whispered a reminder to me, "Don't look up when the ducks circle. Let them light, then pick out a big drake closest to you. And remember, aim right at the water where he sits, not at his head."

I had watched these men do this shot-on-the-water trick before, with devastating results.

When they shot just below the duck, the bottom half of the circular shot pattern ricocheted off the water and hit the duck in the body. The top half would strike the duck directly in the neck and head. If you aimed straight at the duck's head, half of the pattern would go high of your mark. I learned a lot from men who had spent two, three, and even four decades in the woods.

I could hear the whistling of duck wings now. I lowered the bill of my camouflage cap a little and cut my eyes left and right, trying to pick them up. There they were! Banking out to the left. This morning they were going to land on my side of the blind.

"Cock your gun," Dad whispered. "Get ready."

There were nine of them. Big mallards. They locked up, fifty yards out, sailed in and dropped to ten feet above the decoys, and suddenly started to climb out.

"Don't shoot, don't shoot!" someone hissed. "They'll come around."

The ducks were checking out the ice and circling back out, not very high, banking in the harsh rays of the dawn and heading straight back. As a group they flared their wings, dropped their orange webbed feet, and glided to a stop twenty yards from where my right cheek was resting on the freezing cold stock of my new gun. I did not feel the cold. Neither did I feel the kick nor hear the roar of my shot. By some miracle I saw the little .410 pattern melt the bull greenhead closest to shore.

All heck broke loose! Ducks were scrambling for altitude, but more were falling than climbing out. Repeated 12-gauge patterns of No. 4 magnums found their mark. Only two gray hens escaped.

Everyone reloaded. I smiled at Dad as I broke the little over/under open. The spent shell popped out, and I slid a new one in. The smoke of the spent shells hung in the cold air. The sweetest smell every hunter enjoys drifted on a hint of morning breeze: burnt gun powder.

"Get down! There are more coming!"

We all hunched down, hid our faces and tried to make ourselves smaller.

This group of seven passed over for a look-see. Just then one of the ducks we had shot began flopping and carrying-on in the water. The group passing overhead took the commotion below to be feeding ducks. Not wanting to miss out, the little flock locked up, banked sharply, and hit the water so fast I scarcely had time to lift my gun. Everyone was sort of holding his breath while I picked out a duck to shoot.

In spite of my excitement, I got myself together and zeroed in on the closest male that was cruising through the wooden deceivers. I followed the big drake with my barrel. Just as I pulled the trigger, he glided right behind a decoy. Water showered in front of the wooden look-alike. To my horror I saw the decoy's head explode, and my intended target jumped five feet straight up to freedom. Only my duck escaped the withering fire.

Someone down the line asked, "Did we hit one of the decoys?"

I was never so glad to hear the use of the pronoun *we* in my life. Bud, sitting closest to the blind's entrance, grabbed one of the decoy sacks, a burlap seedbag, and waded out to pick up the downed ducks.

He loaded twelve into the sack, but he kept the big bull mallard I killed separate. When he returned to the blind, he handed it in, and each man passed it on to the next until Dad handed it over to me. I beamed with pride. My first duck. I had killed it with my new Christmas shotgun.

It was seven forty-five A.M. I knew the drill. These men would stay until just before lunch. Only a few more ducks would drift in off the lake later in the morning.

I could never sit quietly that long. From past experience I knew they would let me roam the woods on my own until time to leave.

Dad suggested, "Why don't you take the sack of ducks to the Jeep and hunt a little in the woods until time to go? Meet us back here before noon. Be careful, and don't go too far. Okay?"

"Yes, sir," I answered.

As I squeezed out of the blind, each man patted me on the back and said something like,

"Good shot!"

"Good job!"

I was thrilled to be congratulated by these friends of my dad.

I slung the heavy sack over my shoulder and headed up the long green tunnel. I dropped the bulging sack off in the woods near the Jeep, carefully laying my beautiful drake on top. I smoothed all his feathers back into perfect position. A patch of sunlight struck his iridescent feathers, and the metallic emerald color on his head shimmered as it turned from green to black, and back to gleaming green. Dropping a fresh round into the .410 barrel, I headed out to see if I could find a rabbit huddled into its warm bed this frosty morning.

Two-to three-hundred yards up in the woods I came to a narrow, but deep, feeder creek. I knew by instinct I had been paralleling the shore of the lake and this creek was deeper than the original because the water was backing up from the flooded lake. It was too wide to jump across. I did not want to continue walking up to find a better crossing. I picked out a nice, straight poplar tree about ten inches around. I decided I would be like the pioneers. I'd cut it down, let it fall over the creek, and cross it as a footbridge.

I used my hatchet to cut a wedge out on the creek side, about two feet off the ground. After about ten minutes I had hacked deep enough, and then started on the other side. The work was making me warmer, but my feet were still very cold.

It was only another fifteen minutes until I thought the cut in the soft poplar was deep enough. I set the hatchet next to my gun, still propped against a big oak, and pushed on the poplar until it began to rock. When it swayed back toward me and started returning toward the creek, I gave it all I had. It hung just for a second, then snapped at the deep-cut wedges and with a sharp crack fell perfectly across the creek. I looked with satisfaction at my handiwork, picked up my gun, returned the hatchet to the holder on my belt, and scurried over the water to the other side.

As I jumped off the tree's trunk, a rabbit that had been sitting tight in its bed under a nearby cedar tree had stood about all the excitement it could. It jumped up and started toward the woods. I was a little slow getting the gun to my shoulder, but I saw a patch of fur fly from the rabbit's rear end as it streaked up the hill. I reloaded on the run, and followed the rabbit until it ducked into a mammoth kudzu patch. I saw where he ducked in. I was confident he was hit pretty bad, so I began to pick my way through the mess of twisted vines.

The out-of-control choke weed, as kudzu is called, had completely engulfed one of the biggest, deepest, gullies I had ever seen. Let me repeat, this was a rough part of the county. When talking about a gully in Todd's Quarter, you have to think big. Some folks would say that it was so rough, this part of the county was just holding the rest of the world together.

I had seen some impressive gullies, and this one was at the top of the list. I had a pretty good sighting on where the hurt rabbit had stopped, so I waded on through the brown, brittle leaves and vines that had been burned by the winter's chill.

I had marked the rabbit near where the jungle of vines had smothered a five-foot-tall tree. As I got closer, the dying rabbit squirmed. I quickly stooped down and grabbed it by its hind legs. As taught by my dad to insure a quick, clean kill, I whacked it over the head with the heavy barrel of my gun. It died. As I stopped to lay my gun down and put the rabbit on my belt, a movement out of the corner of my eye stopped me in my tracks.

It took a moment for me to realize what I was looking at. With a lot of forethought, someone had constructed a crude arch into which an old window sash had been placed. A piece of rusty tin was bent over it, forming a two-foot hood over the window. The kudzu had covered it all.

I got down on my knees and eased up to the window. My breathing was shallow and rapid. I instinctively knew I should not be here. I was scared, but drawn as if by some overpowering curiosity to see this strange thing.

Once I was out of the bright sunlight and in the shadow of the kudzu-covered arch, I could see clearly through the dusty window panes into a cleverly constructed room.

The floor was wooden, but the walls were formed by the gully. It was much like a large shed had been built to straddle the narrow gully so rainwater would flow under the raised plank floor. Rusted, corrugated tin formed the roof. The non-native, extremely invasive kudzu, known to grow over a foot in a day's time, covered the entire structure. From five feet away no one would suspect that a still operated there. Two men were sitting on low, wooden benches. By the light of kerosene lanterns, I could make out some five-gallon tins and quart jars lined up on the floor. There, close by, was another big, black pot just like Aunt Addie's.

My heart stopped when I realized what I was witnessing!

The men were carefully arranging a half-dozen quart jars filled with moonshine in a circle in the bottom of each five-gallon tin. There was about one inch of space between each glass jar. They were pouring fresh-made lard between and over the jars. Several five-gallon tins had already been filled. Those tins had a smooth surface of white, cooled lard right below the tin's lip. This process insured the jars of illegal liquor were well-protected from breakage and completely camouflaged. It looked like five gallons of Aunt Addie's prime lard.

I was shaking. I knew I needed to run. This was a danger-ous place. I had to go fast and get away from what I had seen. I started to rise, but froze with terror as I felt cold steel pressed on my neck. I heard the unmistakable metallic click of the hammer cocking on a gun. I was so frightened I messed in my pants. I could feel and smell the warm liquid oozing down my legs.

"What the hell you doing there? Turn around! Whatcha doing?" a gruff voice demanded.

I was trembling violently. Barely able to look over my shoul-der, I couldn't speak a word. I turned my head. I was looking up the twin, dime-size holes of a double-barrel shotgun. It was held by a relatively young man. He had a two-day-old beard, and his unkempt blond hair was sticking out of a dirty, navy blue baseball cap. He wore a heavy, blue denim jacket and jeans.

"Why, you're just a kid! What the hell you doing out here?" he demanded again. I could not force my mouth to move. I was scared to death. Embarrassed, I willed myself not to cry, but I was just before losing the battle.

The gun the man was aiming at my neck was weaving pretty good, and his hands were shaking almost as much as mine. The forefinger of his right hand was inside the trigger guard and rest-ing on the trigger. This did not make me feel any better.

"I ought to shoot you right now. You got no business down here. If one of my brothers was out here, 'stead of me, you'd be dead already." He was talking fast. He looked over his shoulder as if expecting somebody.

He lowered the gun a little so it was pointed at my feet. "Guess you're pretty scared," he said as he looked at my britches. "Look, you better be scared! If I catch you telling anybody about this I'm coming to get you! I know where you stay in town. You understand?" he demanded.

With the gun pointed somewhere other than at my head, I managed a weak nod.

"Boy, you stink! Take that peashooter of yours, and get out of here, and never come back! Remember, I'll find you if you tell. You'll be sorry you ever crossed me. You hear?"

As I bent to pick up my gun, I glanced into the window. Two upturned faces not five feet away were staring at me through the dusty panes. Startled, I jumped back, tripped over the vines, scrambled up, and flew out of there. The faces of the three Eubanks brothers were burned into my memory forever.

My mind was racing as fast as my legs were running. The rabbit that hung on my belt was splattering blood all over my right leg. My stomach churned, and I smelled like I had had diarrhea for two days.

Now that I could never let the men back in the blind know what I had seen, how was I to explain my sad condition?

When I got to the tree where I had crossed the deep creek, I was completely out of breath. I fell to my knees and threw up until I was only heaving. My head was spinning. I was burning up and thought I was going to pass out. I needed something cold on my face. I set the gun down and leaned over to scoop up some of the water out of the flooded creek. The cold water helped, and I began to calm down a little.

An idea hit me. I did not know if I was man enough to pull it off, but saw no other way out. I crossed the log. I propped my gun against the big oak tree. I took the rabbit off of my belt along with my hatchet and laid them beside my gun. I walked over to the creek, looked once more at the deep, freezing water, held my nose, and jumped in.

For the second time in less than fifteen minutes, I was certain I was going to die. I did not know that water could be that cold. It rendered me nearly helpless. Every muscle in my body locked up. My jaw muscles froze. I could not holler for help. My arms and legs would not listen to my brain. If the creek had been a foot deeper I would have drowned. Luckily, as I emerged from being two feet under the water, I could stand on my tiptoes and gulp precious air. Somehow I struggled up the bank, gasping.

I was so cold. My wet clothes were becoming stiff. I grabbed my gun, rabbit, and little hatchet, and tore out for the duck blind.

I was so cold I could not feel my toes. By the time I reached the blind, I was crying. I had lost my cap, and ice was forming in my hair. The temperature was still not out of the twenties.

The men took one look at me and poured out of the blind, leaving the decoys behind. We rushed up the gully. I showed them where the ducks were. Dad stripped off my soaking jacket and shirt and bundled me in his big, warm, wool coat. We all piled into the Jeep. The motor raced, and we started up the frozen road. When we got to the gate, Dad jumped out to open it. I looked out the window and was looking straight into the glaring eyes of the three men I had fled from. They just stood there, close by the gate we had to pass through. Clint, the youngest one, still had the shotgun in the crook of his arm. As we pulled through the gate, he patted it with his left hand. I began to cry again.

With the heater blasting on high and Dad's dry coat warming me, I began to realize I was not going to freeze to death. I had narrowly escaped being shot and possibly drowning. By the time we got home, I had convincingly lied about falling off the log footbridge. In the confusion, no one seemed to notice or comment on any lingering bad odor or the fact that my gun, hatchet, and rabbit were all dry.

Thank the Lord, Mom was at the grocery store when we got home. Dad got me undressed and started a hot shower. Into the washing machine went my clothes. Once out of the shower, I was warmed up in a dry flannel shirt and clean jeans. A cup of hot chocolate helped too. I was feeling better, still secretly terrified, but better.

Dad sat me down. He made me look right at him when he explained to me that we did not need to let Mom know about me falling in the creek. We agreed it was best never to tell her. She might put an end to our hunting trips if she knew. Moms, he explained, are funny that way.

We never told. For over sixty years it was our secret.

I did not return to Aunt Addie's that year. The duck season closed in the middle of February. I had pretty regular nightmares for a while. To keep the secret, Dad would come comfort me before Mom could even wake up. As he sat on my bed, he would be sure I was good and awake, pat me on the back, and I would be fine for a couple more weeks. The bad dreams gradually receded over time.

Two years passed.

One fall day while I was with Dad and his hunting friends, they decided to work on the blind at Aunt Addie's. When we pulled into the yard, things looked pretty much normal. Aunt Addie was tending the outside fire. Percy, the older son, and his dad, fresh back from jail, were working under the hood of their 1949 Ford.

One of Dad's friends glanced over, waved at Aunt Addie as we passed through, and casually said as he looked at the Ford, "Fastest doggone car in the county."

As we drove along, he continued, "Those might be sorry boys, but they flat know how to soup up an engine. They gonna get themselves in big trouble though if they keep picking at the Feds. Their operation's gotten pretty big. People are starting to talk about it. Bill Hassle over at Tucker's store is not known for being tight-lipped. He told me he's setting out five fifty-pound bags of sugar a week at that old barn up the road from Aunt Addie's place."

We all heard the familiar signal of the .22 rifle's crack as we drove down the dirt road through a shower of orange, yellow, and crimson autumn leaves.

Two weeks later, the fur hit the fan, as they say. Seems there had been a change in personnel. There was a new ATF captain in charge of upper South Carolina. Word about the Eubanks boys had gotten around. The new captain had apparently taken it on as a personal project to round up the Eubanks and put them all in jail. This fellow, out of the state capitol in Columbia had obtained some extra men and enlisted the less-than-enthusiastic local authorities. On several occasions they tried to catch Clint Eubanks hauling a load of moonshine. Clint and the souped-up black '49 Ford were making quite a reputation in the upper part of the county.

He and his two older brothers ran their Ford on the dirt tracks at the Saturday night races. They were becoming quite the favorites among the local race fans. It was said on a cold night you could hear that car for over a mile as it climbed up the grade from Aunt Addie's with Clint working the gears through the sharp switchbacks. Folks said nobody could catch that car when Clint was driving, nobody on or off the track.

The law was becoming a nuisance though. The Eubanks boys were used to making deliveries on time and without a lot of hassle. Cash was flowing in. No one was really getting hurt, but now these new guys from ATF were putting on the squeeze. The story on the street was the boys had gotten tired of the heat and decided to make a point.

Next thing we heard, all heck had broken loose. The new captain had gotten really angry and had vowed to nail those boys' hides to the jailhouse wall.

Seems Wilbur, the brains in the Eubanks family, had laid a trap for the out-of-town lawman. Wilbur had put the word out that the boys would be making a special run on Thursday night coming, due to growing demand on their normal Friday route.

The ATF captain had bought the lie and enlisted the local sheriff and his men. Three police cars were positioned at the top of the grade coming out of Todd's Quarter. For hours the men stood around the three police cars, smoking, twirling the cylinders in their pistols around, and telling tales.

Sure enough, on Thursday, about one o'clock in the morning, down in the valley in Aunt Addie's yard, the '49's motor rumbled to life. The officers tossed their cigarettes in the ditch and piled into the cars. Each car, with lights switched off, was backed into the bushes.

Wilbur had sent Percy to the railroad crossing where the Columbia, Newberry, and Laurens (CN&L) train, better known as the Crooked, Noisy, and Late, crossed Lake Greenwood Road. He had armed Percy with a headlight out of an old Mack B model truck, a twelve-volt battery, and a large air horn off a wrecked 1953 Kenworth road tractor. Percy was well coached on his role in the unfolding plot.

The men waiting in the police cars could hear the Eubanks' car roaring toward them. Their radios crackled as the ATF captain barked orders for the two local cars to follow him as backup. Under no circumstances were they to interfere with him in the lead car. They were there for assistance only. The sheriff's deputies rolled their eyes as they looked over at each other.

Clint was just about at the top of the grade and shifting gears expertly as he leveled out on the Cold Point Road. The speedometer was climbing toward eighty as the cool, dense night air carried the hum of the meticulously tuned engine.

He was very alert. Every nerve was as tight as a banjo string. He downshifted and let off the accelerator a bit. Just as he came around the last sharp curve, lights from all three police cars flashed on from both sides of the road.

The captain gunned his car and tried to jump out in front of the '49 Ford to head it off. Clint, however, had been too quick. He hit the brakes, and the revenue car shot in front of Clint with such speed it crossed the road and almost wound up in the deep ditch on the opposite side. Clint immediately cut his lights off, swung the Ford to the right, and put the accelerator to the floor. Gravel flew everywhere as the tires of the powerful flathead V-8 engine spun on the tar-and-gravel road. The two local police cars, now side by side in the middle of the road, were getting peppered with marble-size gravel. They couldn't see a thing and were almost run over by the captain's car as it fishtailed back into the road behind Clint and in front of the backup officers.

Clint knew this road well. He knew he had four miles of near straightaway before the crossing. The Ford leaped as it finally got full traction, and the chase was on.

Clint wanted to keep the lead chase car at a safe distance behind, but he needed them to be able to just barely see where he was as he drew the ATF men into the trap. The captain, not knowing the road, had to run with his headlights on. The rotating lights on top of all three cars threw shafts of red light across rolling pastures and curious cows. Sirens wailed through the quiet countryside.

A half-mile from the CN&L railroad crossing, Clint slowed to sixty. The captain, driving hard, thought he was gaining on the Ford and put his foot into the firewall.

"We'll get him now, sergeant!" he yelled over the noise of the siren and wind whistling through the open window.

"We're gaining fast," he yelled again as he gripped the steering wheel with both hands. The captain had a broad grin on his face. His sergeant, sitting next to him, had a pipe clenched tight in his teeth, and he was holding on for dear life. They were running at nearly a hundred.

Clint crossed the tracks carefully. He looked out the driver's side window and spotted Percy waiting in the shadows. Clint now cut on his lights. He wanted everyone behind him to be totally focused on the Ford. He was down to forty miles an hour now and mainly watching in his rearview mirror.

When the captain's car got within thirty yards of the crossing, it was traveling over ninety miles an hour. Percy, standing just off the pavement, with expert timing, quickly flipped the switch of the powerful truck headlight and sat down hard on the air horn. He rushed toward the captain's car with the blinding light.

As the captain reached the crossing, he heard the deafening horn and saw the huge, bright light not ten yards away and coming fast. He was certain he was only a split second from being run over by the oncoming train. He hit the brakes and jerked the steering wheel as hard as he could to the right. The car hit the protruding tracks and became airborne, landing hard on the rough, right-hand shoulder. It plowed through a barbed wire fence, busting a good dozen sturdy, cedar fence posts off at ground level as if they were matchsticks.

The two backup cars saw the impending danger just in time to lock their brakes and skid to a stop, one on the left-hand shoulder and one facing straight down the railroad tracks. A deputy in that car later testified he thought he saw a lone man running down the track, just beyond the reach of his headlights.

The captain's car, still on the hook of the wrecker from Wesley Taylor's Gulf station when people started arriving on the square to go to work the next morning, was a total loss. A large cedar post stuck out of the grill. It had jammed the radiator and engine block back into the front seat. Tangled, rusty barbed wire was rolled up around both axles.

The captain suffered a broken nose and a badly damaged ego. The sergeant riding in the car had miraculously survived with only two front teeth missing when the pipe he was smoking smashed into the dashboard. He had swallowed the two teeth. He was lucky he had not swallowed the pipe, too.

All of this and the details of the night's episode were told and retold by the local deputies in the chase cars. The entire town knew the whole story by lunch. What people didn't know, they just made up.

This began a few weeks of an all-hands-on-deck effort from the ATF. Dad and his friends agreed we would hunt some of our other duck spots for a while and let things cool down some.

One Sunday morning in February when we arrived at church, I heard a member of Dad's Sunday school say "They caught Clint last night on the Todd's Quarter Road. Took five cars to hem that Ford up, but now they have him in jail."

All Dad said was, "It was bound to happen."

I did not say a thing about my experience in the woods two-and-a-half years earlier. And I never would.

Monday afternoon after Dad got off work, he said, "Let's ride downtown."

We slowly drove around the square a couple of times. Dad was looking for something, but I did not know what. On the next slow trip around, he spied the sheriff coming out of the west side door of the courthouse. Dad eased the car over and pulled alongside the sheriff just as he stepped off the sidewalk. Dad had his window down and he asked, "Hey, Walter, what's the story on the Eubanks boy?"

"Those ATF boys finally caught him on the Todd's Quarter Road. He was doing over a hundred on that long straightaway at the Owens' Farm. The cops had commandeered Red's tractor and hay wagon and had them blocking that concrete bridge. They said the kid did some fancy driving just to keep from going over the railing."

"Just finished the preliminary hearing. Judge had to let him go with only a speeding ticket, though."

"Let him go?" Dad questioned.

"Yeah," the sheriff said, "the only thing the ATF guys found he was hauling in the trunk of the car was five-gallon tins of Aunt Addie's lard." He added with a sly smile, "Most men around here say it's the best dang lard ever made."

Ten Was The Deal

As I stood chest deep in the damp hole anticipating the next shot, the memory of the man who had dug my grave flowed as swiftly through my subconscious as the small river that was running in front of me now.

It all began in this watery wilderness late last winter, a year ago.

The Switch Bush Swamp, as I called it, was perhaps my favorite duck hunting spot throughout my teenage years. It belonged to Jack Whitaker. Mr. Whitaker owned about three hundred acres up on the Princeton Road, about six miles from our house on the edge of Laurens, a small town in upstate South Carolina. Jack was a big farmer, a good friend of my granddad, and he had a passion for high-blooded black Angus cows.

The bulk of Jack's cattle farm was U-shaped. Princeton Road followed a ridge almost the entire length of the U. The whole farm sloped gradually away from the road, ran down a huge pasture to Rabon Creek and ended in a large swamp.

You could ride up Princeton Road in the fall and the winter at daybreak or dusk and look way down that pasture as you circled the ridge. If you knew what to look for, you could see big ducks, mallards and blacks, rising from or landing in this waterfowl paradise.

Jack Whitaker was obsessed with the thought that someone might accidentally shoot one of his prize black beauties. He never allowed anyone to hunt his bottoms. No one, that is, but me. In the 1930s when land was cheap but money was tight, Granddad had helped Jack buy part of the land that made up Jack's farm. Now that I could drive legal, at fourteen years of age in 1959, Granddad had taken me with him to meet Jack. He introduced me. After a thorough set of instructions from both men on the dos and don'ts of hunting around cows, I finally received the go-ahead from Mr. Jack to hunt his swamp and surrounding bottom land.

While there were more ducks in some of the other rivers, this one was my favorite spot. No one but me ever messed with those ducks for the five or six years that I hunted there. I never heard another shot or saw evidence that another person had ever walked that way. I had the place to myself.

As the long, sloping pasture entered the swamp, Rabon Creek made a large curve – high ground on the inside and large swamp on the outside of that curve. The ducks loved this area. It was wide open, and I guess they felt safe landing here. I would go to this spot morning after morning, stand at the edge of the hard-woods, and watch dozens of mallards circle out over the swamp, hook back over the river, and light in this bend.

They would then swim out of the river and into the swamp to feed on the little blue switch bush berries off and on all day. The ducks loved these berries. A visiting cousin from Atlanta once asked me what switch bushes were. This question came after I was excitedly telling him that there was a bumper crop of switch bush berries, and the ducks were really piling in to eat them.

I took him to the back window of the kitchen and pointed to a big bush in the backyard. I said, "You know, it's those bushes your mom gets the switch off of when she's going to wear you out." He looked at me like I was from another planet. I guessed his mom used some other kind of bush for switches in Atlanta.

Near the big, wide curve in the swamp there was not a bit of cover anywhere to hide in, and the tallest vegetation was no more than a foot high. I had spent several late winter mornings when there was snow on the ground, watching, but I had no luck getting a shot. Absent any cover, I could never get close enough. The later the season got, the more big ducks poured into that one spot. Finally, the season closed, and I had not ever gotten a shot at those particular ducks.

All through February and March I thought about how to set up on those ducks that used the curve. By April I had a grand plan in mind. What I needed was a pit dug at ground level within twenty yards of the edge of the river. I could get down in it and not be visible from above the ground and the foot-tall swamp grasses. I had read about pit blinds for goose hunting, but I had never seen one before.

The image in my mind from what I had read was a hole about three feet by six feet, deep enough to stand in. What I needed was a grave!

In the small town where I lived you knew just about everyone and what they did for a living. I decided I needed a grave dug, and I knew Big Henry was a grave digger. Big Henry worked for Kennedy Mortuary. He dug all the graves for all the funerals in town. Kennedy Mortuary owned no machine for this job, so Big Henry, working alone, dug them with pick and shovel. Henry got his name honestly. He was big. The biggest man, black or white, in town or, for that matter, the biggest man that I had ever seen anywhere. I knew Henry well. Besides digging graves, Henry had the best pack of rabbit dogs in upper South Carolina. My dad paid for all the food and occasional trips to the vet, Henry kept the dogs, and we all hunted together. Henry, his three young boys, my granddad, Dad, and me.

One day while I was helping Big Henry and his boys put up the dozen or so short-legged beagles and feed them, I confided in Henry. I needed him to dig me a grave in Jack Whitaker's bottoms, preferably before fall came around. I hurriedly told him my plan.

As we fed the dogs, Big Henry listened and smiled. He said he got ten dollars to dig a grave. "I don't 'spect yo daddy gonna pay no ten dollars for me to dig a grave for you to shoot ducks out of."

I told him I didn't believe Daddy needed to know about the grave. I would help Big Henry all summer at the cemetery, if he would dig the grave for me. I knew he hated fussing with the folding wooden chairs and wreaths of flowers. Henry was a dirt-moving man. Putting the chairs in neat rows, and unloading, and arranging the flowers were not his favorite parts of the job.

As we finished feeding the dogs I made my pitch. I'd help with ten funerals, one dollar credit for each funeral. Then he'd dig me one grave before duck season. A fair deal, I emphasized. Big Henry thought about this as we walked back to his two-story house with the chickens running in and out from under the full-length front porch.

"Never have any problem with termites," Henry said.

I thought I had misheard him. "Whadya say?"

"The chickens, running loose like that, go under the house and eat up the termites that try to go up the rock pillars. Never have any problem with termites."

I did not see any connection between this and grave digging, but politely said, "That's very interesting," and hurriedly added, "What do you think about the grave, Henry?"

At last he said yes, but I had to put the chairs out, take them up afterwards, and put the flowers on the grave at ten funerals before he would start digging. As an afterthought Henry said he thought we'd better keep this arrangement to ourselves. He was not too sure what Dad would say about him digging me a grave. I assured him I would not be telling a soul.

I spent all summer worrying that not enough folks were going to die. Ten funerals was a lot of dead people for our little town, and I was racing the calendar. I kept close tabs on the obituaries in *The Advertiser*, as our local paper was named. The papers were sold for five cents on the street corners of the square every Wednesday.

By late August I was a nervous wreck. Only six people had died all summer. Everyone was very healthy that summer, it seemed. However, September turned out to be a bonanza. Three funerals in three weeks! I was probably the only person in town who was so happy and relieved, secretly of course.

Being an eternal optimist, as all hunters are, I had, for several weeks leading up to September, been very busy building a big wooden box to put down into the grave Big Henry and I were going to dig.

I had gotten two old oak pallets from the glass plant where my dad and granddad worked. This glass bottle and jar manufacturing plant used four-foot by four-foot oak pallets to stack the crates of bottles on. These pallets were sort of scrap and ended up in all types of projects around the county – hog pens, rabbit gums, and just plain firewood. These two I cut to size to be the floor of my duck blind. Next, I built up the sides and ends to about five feet high. Finally, I constructed folding doors that hinged at the top. They would cover up the entire box when closed.

On several occasions my dad, returning home after work, asked what it was I was building in the backyard. I said it was going to be a duck blind. My dad looked at it the way dads always do when viewing young boys' summertime building projects – glad I was home and doing something constructive, but doubtful of the final outcome.

I got the duck blind completed, and after many dry runs in the backyard to ensure that it was neither too shallow nor too deep, I took the whole thing apart, numbering each part as I went. After all, when the time came I would have to get the whole affair across Rabon Creek, piece by piece, and put it back together again.

On September 20, a Friday afternoon, as I was placing the flowers on top of the ninth fresh mound of dirt, and Henry was loading his tools into the mortuary's old Chevrolet truck, he said, "What about tomorrow?"

"But I have one more grave to do. Ten was the deal," I said.

"It's been dry for two weeks, and the river ought to be low. We better go now, and you can do the tenth grave some time later," Big Henry said.

"What time you want to leave?" I said.

"I'll pick you up at your house at 6:30 in the morning. You bring us some sandwiches, and I'll get us some drinks," Henry said.

I'm convinced God made September Saturdays just for young boys. A sort of payback for piano lessons, family reunions, and trips to the dentist. This one was a honey – cool, crisp, and clear. Four peanut butter and grape jelly sandwiches in a brown paper sack, nails, hammer, saw, and the knocked-down duck blind were ready to load when the long-bed Chevrolet one-ton truck pulled into our yard.

Big Henry and I loaded and started up Princeton Road. I undid the barbed wire gap at the top of the pasture to let Henry drive through. I carefully replaced the gap. I was well tutored on the proper hunter's etiquette of not climbing fences, but rolling under, making double sure all gates were refastened, and not running the farmer's cows. We kept to the very edge of the tree line and eased the old truck down the pasture toward Rabon Creek.

Big Henry, like all country folks who spend a lot of time outdoors, had picked a good day. The river, about twenty yards wide, was down to knee-deep, and the ground had dried out, so we were able to pull to within a few yards of the big curve. As Henry looked across the river, I pointed out where I thought the pit should be. We unloaded Henry's tools: one square-face shovel, one mattock, and one long, coarse file. Henry took off his heavy shoes, tied the laces together, hung them around his neck, rolled up his pants legs, and waded across. I followed and began to make the first of many trips across, carrying pieces of the knocked-down blind.

When I got across, Henry had put his shoes back on – no socks – and was sharpening his shovel with that big file. Henry laid the shovel facedown over a sycamore log and stroked the coarse file across the bottom edge of his shovel a few times, always pushing the file, never dragging it back. After a dozen strokes Henry held the shovel up, and the morning sun glinted off the sharp, fresh edge.

"How big you want the hole?" Henry asked.

"I've never seen you dig but one size," I said, "so I built the blind to fit – you know three feet by seven feet, but let's make this one only five feet deep. That's as deep as I made the blind 'cause I can't shoot out of anything deeper."

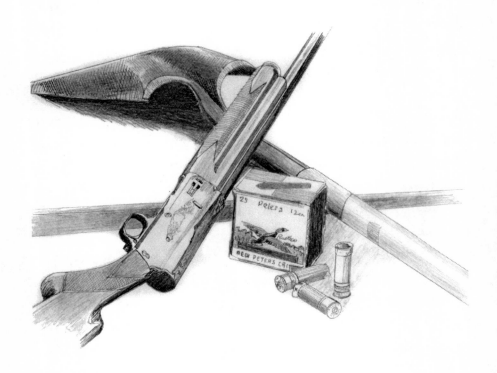

Henry picked up the shovel, cleared away the grass, and started to dig. I had watched Big Henry do this most of the summer, but I still was amazed at his strength. I was pretty strong for my age and had to dig holes for one reason or another around the yard at home. Even my best efforts would result in standing on the shovel, pushing about a fourth of it into the ground, bending it back, and actually only moving about a double handful of dirt. It was hard work and slow going.

That was not how Big Henry usually used a shovel. When Henry put the shovel into the ground, it went down until his foot rested on the top of the earth. Every shovelful was the same shape – wide as the shovel, long as the shovel, and ten inches thick. They never varied. It was something else to see, and I never got tired of watching. The sides were perfectly straight, the corners square, and the bottom level. No machine could have done it as precisely.

By the time I had all the lumber across, Henry was knee-deep in the hole. Shirt off, pants legs still rolled up, Henry was moving dirt – steady, no talking, no breaks – just moving dirt.

By ten o'clock I told Henry to hold up. He was getting pretty deep and I was afraid he might be going for a regular-size grave. Henry climbed out, and I climbed in. It was the first time I had ever been in a grave, and I felt a little funny down there. I knew I'd have trouble getting out if Henry was not there. Sides straight and slick as glass. I shouldered an imaginary gun and swung left to right. With nothing in the grave to stand on, I would not have been able to shoot lower than three feet above the rim. The pallets that made up the floor were half a foot thick, so I knew we were about right. I told Henry we were deep enough.

Two hours later we had most of the blind reassembled down in the grave. We sat on the fresh earth mound and ate our lunch.

When we finished our Cokes we both turned the heavy, light green six-and-a-half-ounce bottles over and looked at the name of the city and state molded into the bottoms. Both had an LGW, the symbol for Laurens Glass Works, pressed in the center, showing that they had been made right there in our town. As was traditional, we bet each other that our bottle had been made for a bottling plant farthest away from our town. In addition to the LGW on the bottom, the name of the town where the bottle was going was also spelled out in the glass.

The one farther away won the bet, and the loser bought the Cokes next time. My bottle read Asheville, North Carolina, and Big Henry's read Greenville, South Carolina.

Big Henry laughed and said he had never been to Asheville, North Carolina, but he 'spected it was further than Greenville, where his sister lived. He said, "I owe you one."

Big Henry looked at the bottom of his bottle one more time and said, "Seems like most of my bottles been no further than I have."

Getting up, Henry said, "Burning daylight. Let's get the rest of your duck blind down in the hole."

We fastened the sides, and then finally we put on the top. I was very grateful everything fit with only a few minor adjustments. I helped scatter the dirt all around the blind and closed up the two doors to keep the rain out some. We waded back across Rabon Creek. It was 3:00 P.M.

When we got on the other side we loaded the tools. As Henry and I sat on the tailgate of the truck and put our shoes back on, we both looked across the clear two-foot-deep river and commented that the blind just might work. Henry suggested that after a rain or two to settle the dirt I might scatter some swamp grass around the blind. About halfway up the pasture I took one last look out the rear window. I was pretty pleased with myself. I could hardly see where we had been.

September and the first two weeks of October passed with no thought of ducks. It was dove season, and I hunted with Dad and Granddad every Saturday. In late October I checked on the blind and did as Henry had suggested. I scattered some swamp grass, now turning brown after the frost and planted some low bushes on the side of the blind away from the river to help break up the outline.

Duck season would not begin until Thanksgiving, but on several occasions I was at the wood line overlooking the curve. I was excited to see the early-flying summer ducks, that we called woodies, light within two dozen yards of the blind.

Since hunting season had opened I had not worked a funeral, and I was feeling a little guilty. Henry had not said anything, and I knew he wouldn't. He would understand. I would get that last funeral done just as soon as hunting season wrapped up.

Opening day of duck season I hunted with Granddad and Dad at Buzzard's Roost, probably the best duck hunting place in our county and also the best kept secret. The following two Saturdays we shot at Burton Pond and below McPherson's Bridge. All these were wonderful duck hunting spots that were regulars on our early season list. When the Saturday before Christmas came, Dad and Granddad had been invited to hunt the Brick Yard ponds owned by Greenwood Mills. Since I was not invited to this most prestigious event, I planned my first trip of the season to the new blind in Jack Whitaker's bottoms.

It was very cold, but clear as a bell, when I pulled off Princeton Road and parked. I had an old M-1 ammo bag that came from the Army/Navy store. I put it over my shoulder, dropped in a box of Peter's high brass No. 4s, took the Browning A5 12-

gauge that had been a gift from my dad six years before, and headed down the pasture. The moon was only two days into new. It was still pretty dark, so I walked out in the pasture farther from the tree line than I would have had it been daylight. I timed my trip so I would arrive at the blind at 6:45 A.M. The first ducks would fly at 7 o'clock sharp, just as the little birds began to make their morning sounds. Fifteen minutes would be all the time I needed to get the doors off the blind, fix a few bushes around the edges for added cover, and load up.

Granddad and Dad had taught me many hunts ago that nothing was going to happen until 7:00 A.M. You would only lose the warmth from walking to your blind if you had to stand around in the dark with nothing to do but wait on the ducks.

When I got to the river the water was up some, and I waded very slowly across. The water as it pushed against my boots bulged up some on the upriver side and came to within an inch or so of my hip boot tops. I knew it would get shallower as I approached the inside of the curve, so a few extra careful minutes in the deepest part was a small price to pay for warm, dry feet.

I cut it a little close and barely had the two tops off and stowed against the back wall of the blind when a pair of summer ducks swished overhead only ten feet above the blind. The pink of the eastern sky lit the far bank. The towhees and cardinals began their morning caroling, and the soft quacks of a small group of big ducks could be heard coming from downriver.

In our part of the county, all the big ducks roosted on Greenwood Lake and would come from downriver. The summer ducks roosted in the flooded timber along the small creeks and would come from upriver most of the time. Because it is hilly in our part of the country, you can always hear ducks before you can see them. Having heard their approach, I now saw the mallards' light-colored breasts glowing in the darkened sky as the sun struck them even before it was completely clear of the horizon.

There were six of them, and they passed over pretty high. I was a little worried as they flew over. I caught a glimpse of them bank. I kept my head still, but cut my eyes as far as possible. I had learned long ago that you can't kill a duck until it is within thirty to forty yards, and it won't ever get that close if you keep twisting your neck and head and showing your white face. Keeping still, as hard as that was, was the only way.

The half dozen had their wings cupped now. They were losing altitude quickly. I thought they were going to come straight in when, at the last minute and a little out of range, they pulled up and headed out over the pasture, talking to each other about whatever ducks talk about when they are flying forty-five miles an hour and trying to decide where to have breakfast.

I held my breath. At last someone in the crowd must have said this looks like the right place. They dipped their wings, banked sharply, and never took another wing beat. They were cupped up, sailing in with the winter sun showcasing the tan tummies, yellow beaks, iridescent green heads, and bright orange feet. At fifty yards out, they banked slightly to line up with the curve and passed the blind, ten feet off the water and thirty yards out. They looked as if they were frozen in time, and my first shot was behind. They backpedaled at my first movement and my shot. I caught up with two big greenheads with the second and third shots. Both colorful males fell with a satisfying splash and quickly drifted into a big brush top against the far bank.

Within ten minutes a single mallard hen came in, much lower this time. Without much reconnaissance, she lit upriver about sixty yards. After looking around, making sure all was as she had left it the evening before, she noisily straightened her feathers and sailed on the current down into the curve.

She purposely swam to the inside of the curve where there was very little current and began nibbling at the grass on the river's edge. A few minutes passed, and I watched her. She was not fifteen yards away. I could hear her snapping her bill together as she rapidly stripped seeds from the heads of the tall yellow grass.

Long before I heard or saw them, she tuned up and began calling to her friends that were rapidly approaching from down-river. As a pair of mallards appeared over the tree line, the gray hen convinced them that no look-see was necessary, and they locked up. I shot the right-hand female two feet off the water and the big drake about two wing beats into his climb out. The Judas hen, with much protest, flew out without damage except to her reputation.

I quickly scurried out of the blind, ran down the bank, got ahead of the last two ducks and waded out midway to catch them as they floated by. I returned to the blind and put the doors back in place, put a few bushes over the top, and reentered Rabon Creek. I could not help but think how much shallower moving water always seems in the bright morning sun than it does in the dark starlight. I collected the first two ducks and headed home.

I was pleased with myself. My plan had come together, and the work Big Henry and I had done was going to pay off for a long time to come. I determined to take Big Henry two of the nice mallards as soon as I had them cleaned and dressed. As I walked up the long pasture I thought how much Big Henry and his family would like those ducks. They ate a lot of rabbits, and the ducks would make a fine Christmas dinner. I must confess though, I also wanted to brag some on how well the idea had actually worked. I wasn't too sure Big Henry had ever really thought much of the idea.

When I got home I cleaned all four ducks, picked out the two biggest and headed over to where Big Henry lived. When I turned onto Madden Station Road, there were several cars in addition to the mortuary truck parked in front of the house. A white wreath was hanging on the screen door. When I stepped onto the porch a very large lady dressed all in white opened the front door as she headed out.

When she saw me she said, "Why, ain't you Miz Harriett's boy?"

I said I was, and that I came to bring these ducks, as I offered the shallow glass pan.

The lady took it and said, "News sure travels fast. Henry was killed by that drunk only last night, and already half the town has showed up." She left me standing there on the porch and disappeared back into the house. She said over her shoulder that she would see that Miz Harriett's dish would be returned, for sure.

I stood there for several minutes not knowing what else to say or do, and then I turned and slowly walked down the wide wooden steps. A car full of women was just pulling up. Another car was coming up the dirt drive. Halfway across the yard I thought about the rabbit dogs, so I turned and went around back where the large chicken wire dog pen was. As soon as I turned the corner of the house I could see Henry's boys, my Saturday hunting companions, sitting near the dog pen on the tailboard of an old grain drill. The two youngest were crying. Ramsey, the oldest, was just staring at the ground. He only looked up after I had stood there in silence for a full five minutes.

"He's gone," said Ramsey.

"I'm very sorry," I said.

"Momma says I got to be the man of the house and look after things now. I might have to quit school," Ramsey said.

I wondered to myself how my thirteen-and-a-half-year-old friend was exactly supposed to be this replacement with less than twelve hours notice, but instead I asked, "Dogs and chickens been fed?"

We both looked over at the fifteen nearly identical black-and-tan faces lined up inside the chicken wire. "No, but it's past feeding time. Look at 'em. They know he's gone too."

It was true. Instead of jumping on the wire insistently and barking to be let out, each little beagle just sat there, heads cocked in varying poses of questioning.

"Come on," I said, "Let's get started. I'll do the chickens, y'all feed the dogs." Ramsey got the two little ones up and going to help mix the Jim Dandy dog food with water. I poured up a #10 galvanized bucket full of Spartan Mills scratch feed.

As I walked across that broom-brushed yard, scattering the feed to the ever hungry chickens, I grew very sad. Henry really was gone. His death came quickly, unexpected and unwanted. There was no long illness, no getting used to the idea. He was stabbed while trying to break up a knife fight on Back Street.

I was glad I was alone as the warm, salty moisture dropped off my chin. My Southern raising would not have allowed me to wipe my eyes and perhaps show that I was crying. That men don't cry is taught from age three.

"Now, now, don't cry. Big boys don't cry" is repeated often and regularly by Dads and Uncles.

So I slowly walked away from the boys, scattering the chickens' breakfast. I let the tears for my big friend and his boys fall among the wheat and cracked corn.

Later that day I learned that Henry's funeral was to be held late Sunday afternoon. After church on Sunday I went to Moriah Baptist Church. The small graveyard was a typical country church cemetery.

There were a few 150-year-old red cedars at the perimeter, and simple scattered tombstones, some so old they were just big field rocks turned long side up. In front of some of the tomb-stones were a few turned-over containers of long-dead, hand-picked flowers.

The grass was kept cut, there just wasn't much of it. Red clay was showing through. Even on a good day it was a sad place.

It wasn't a good day. A few days before Christmas, it had started out clear and cold. Now a heavy cloud cover laden with moisture had blown in with a fifteen-mile-an-hour northeast wind, and it felt much colder than it really was. The clouds were unusually low, and it looked and felt like it would start sleeting at any time.

In the graveyard behind the small church there was a man sitting on a big, borrowed, yellow machine digging the grave. The little man on the machine was having a hard time getting it right, and it was taking a long time. The hole was too big. There were ragged claw marks from the scoop on the edges and walls. The corners were broken off and had crumbled into the bottom. Unlike the near perfect, hand-dug graves I had seen Henry labor over, this was the worst grave I had ever seen. Standing at a safe distance, I watched a while until he finished. It was late, and he was in a hurry. The funeral would begin in an hour.

As he got off, I walked up to him and asked if I could help him arrange the chairs and flowers. He said sure. He said he was new at this, and they should have sent someone to help him. While the man got the machine parked away from the grave and stored his tools, I began arranging everything. When I finished, the folding wooden chairs were set up in straight rows, and the flowers were properly arranged.

When I had it all ready, the man looked at it and said, "Not bad, you were a lot of help. Here's a dollar for your trouble."

"No," I told him, "but thank you."

As I turned to go, the sleet began to fall. I thought, *After all, ten was the deal.*

Written as a gift for Ashley Faris Patterson, Christmas 2006

Big Possums Walk Late

The Thursday, Friday, and Saturday after the opening day of turkey season my dad, my granddad, and I headed to the lower part of the state. It was our annual hunting trip organized by Granddad. I looked forward to it as much as Christmas morning.

We always stayed with some of my grandfather's friends. They were large landowners who farmed many acres of corn, tobacco, and sunflowers. Early turkey season coincided with planting time, and that was part of the magic of the trip. Acres upon acres of land were being turned over. The freshly tilled earth was like a magnet pulling all the turkeys out of the many swamps and into the open fields. Midmorning and late afternoon you could ride down the sandy, shady dirt roads bordering these big flat fields and see, not dozens of turkeys, but tens of dozens in a single day.

It was at this mecca of South Carolina turkey hunting that we yearly met our two friends and guides, Cecil and his son, Dick. Cecil and Dick were from Chase City, Virginia. They were wonderful woodsmen. Both made their living as tobacco buyers for the Brown & Williamson Tobacco Company. They spent all tobacco season at the auction barns in Williamsburg and Georgetown counties. For years as a young boy my dream was to grow up and be just like Cecil and Dick. It seemed to me they were always either hunting, fishing, or getting ready to go do one or the other.

My dad and I always hunted with Dick, but my granddad and Cecil were inseparable when we went to the Lowcountry. It was never discussed. My granddad and Cecil were going to hunt together. My granddad was getting on up in years and Cecil took great delight and went to tremendous lengths to be sure he and my granddad ended up killing the biggest, hardest to kill turkey of the season. Most of the time they ended up with the bragging rights. Quantity was never an objective. These two old boys were after quality! And year after year they produced!

One year, though, it seemed fate was to give my dad and me the upper hand. I had killed a nice turkey the first day of the hunt. Dad had killed a twenty-pounder on the second day, a really big turkey for this part of South Carolina.

Cecil and Granddad had yet to get their bird. They had worked what they said was a monster for two-and-a-half days. At every meal, we would get long, detailed descriptions of just how big and smart this turkey was.

"Never seen one bigger."

"Smartest turkey we ever fooled with."

On and on it went. They got to calling it the Light Line Turkey because they had seen it most often strutting on the big power line right-of-way that runs through six hundred acres of fourteen-year-old pines.

Our normal schedule was: up at 5:00 A.M., have coffee and a sweet roll, and leave for the first hunt by 6:00. A big country breakfast was served at 9:00, and then you went back hunting from 10:00 to 1:00. Soup and sandwiches were ready when we returned, and a nap followed.

If you had gotten your turkey for the day by lunchtime, you rode miles and miles of dirt roads that afternoon and spotted turkeys for the following day's hunt. Trying to roost a bird at sundown was the last event before a big country supper at 8:00 P.M. The menu called for fried quail and gravy, fried fresh fish, and boiled cabbage, or venison stew. Whatever it was, we were ready for it.

We were at breakfast on the last day, 10:00 A.M. Saturday. Cecil and Granddad had worked the Light Line Turkey for one and a half hours after the turkeys had flown off the roost. Big Boy, however, had smelled a rat and had not come close enough. Cecil was getting very determined at this point and announced to Lees, the plump, smiling camp cook, to fix his and Mr. Johnny's sandwiches. They were not coming in for lunch. They would be staying out until they got their turkey.

I never saw Cecil with a turkey vest in all the years I knew him. Most turkey hunters have their favorite camouflage vest with untold numbers of pockets filled with box calls, slate calls, three or four favorite strikers, diaphragm calls in small individual boxes, crow calls, woodpecker calls, small pruning scissors, too many shotgun shells, year-old candy bars, and a pair of real turkey wings to simulate a hen flying off the roost.

Not Cecil. He must have had fifty turkey calls – maybe more – but he carried them in a small black satchel, almost like an old-fashioned doctor's bag. The turkey calls rattled and clicked when he walked through the woods. You could hear that racket for miles. If I had not seen him call in so many big turkeys, I would have said he was the worst guide ever.

Cecil's wife, Ann, was a dealer of antiques. She would run up on whole collections of turkey calls during her buying trips. Cecil tried them all and faithfully carried them in his bag. Old

Reliable, however, was a four-inch handmade, fifty-year-old wal-nut wonder he carried in his button-down shirt pocket along with a piece of worn slate. Cecil would carefully hold that wooden box in his left hand between his first finger and thumb, take that old piece of slate between the corresponding two fingers of his right hand, and touch the paper-thin lip of the box.

The near-perfect imitation of a desperate, lovesick hen floated through the spring woods causing every male turkey, young or old, to swell his chest, thrust his long slender neck, and boom out in turkey talk, "I love you with all my heart, you are the only one I will ever love. I'm on my way!"

Cecil experimented with many of the calls in that vast inven-tory he carried, but he called turkeys with that one special call.

Fortified by a big breakfast and armed with sandwiches, a cutoff chair for my granddad, his call bag, and a single hen decoy, the two old-timers drove off in Cecil's forest green Chevrolet pickup.

The cutoff chair was Cecil's invention made for and used only by my granddad. Cecil had taken a curved-back wooden captain's chair with arms and cut the legs off so that the back legs were only two inches long. The two front legs he left about two inches longer. When Granddad sat in this chair with a tree at his back, and two or three broken-off myrtle bush branches stuck in the soft ground in front of him, no turkey in the woods would make him out as long as he remained very still.

This unique invention had two additional advantages. Since the ground always slopes up against a tree, the longer front legs made the chair sit level. The arms of the chair let Granddad steady his left elbow so that he could hold his gun up at the ready for a very long time. Being comfortable allowed my granddad the ability to sit motionless until those old Toms came within range.

I always suspected Miss Ann was missing a right expensive antique chair.

Granddad and Cecil discussed strategy all the way back to the power line. Their well-planned, deliberate campaign was designed to outsmart a four-and-a-half-year-old monster of the woods that had already seen every trick in the book. No run-and-gun here. This was a siege.

Cecil positioned Granddad down in his cutoff chair about ten feet inside the pines. The sun would be at their backs as it went down. The hen decoy with a long, slender neck was set twenty feet off to my granddad's left shoulder. The swamp was approximately seventy-five yards off my granddad's right shoulder. Cecil was another twenty feet in the pines and about in line with the decoy.

The plan was for the turkey to spend the heat of the day in the swamp and come to the power line as the day cooled off. The old Tom would then, they hoped, walk right to left past my granddad's position in its approach to the seductive imitation hen. The scheme was to set up, get comfortable, let the woods quiet down, and not make a single call for at least an hour.

Across the power line was a large tract of fourteen-year-old pines. They were set out in long, straight rows and planted on top of two-and-a-half-foot hills that had been rowed up by huge machines after the land was block cut years before. These areas were one-hundred- to three-hundred-acres in size. Every single tree, regardless of size or variety, was cut to the ground and deep-plowed into rows. The young pines were then planted in the top of the rows. The effect was much like a field of planted corn. As the trees grew, they created long, wide tunnels through the pines, carpeted with six-inch-deep pine needles, very open, very straight, and very clean.

The first hour passed. Cecil removed his ancient little call from his shirt pocket and stroked a series of clucks and purrs that would have made a grown man cry. He placed the call down in the pine needles beside him and began the long wait. Twelve noon came, then one o'clock.

Cecil could see my granddad carefully watching the power line and eating his sandwich. Cecil made another impressive plea on his call and then he ate his own lunch.

Two o'clock came, then three, then four. Granddad had long ago slipped into a sound sleep, his 12-gauge lying across the arms of the cutoff chair. Cecil also dozed a little as the shadows started to creep out from the pines onto the power line.

The air began to cool a little. A light breeze stirred. Cecil, with his chin on his chest, slowly raised his eyes and looked at the hen decoy for the hundredth time. He did a double take. The old gobbler was not twenty yards away. He appeared four feet tall. Cecil could see his long, curved spurs, even at that distance. He was full grown with a two-finger-wide, twelve-inch-long beard.

The old gobbler pecked at the clover that had been planted last fall and took a step closer. His path, if he continued, was straight down the power line, right past Granddad.

Cecil could hear Granddad's steady breathing and started looking for a pinecone or anything to throw. Nothing was in reach, so he slipped a hand in the call bag and slowly pulled out a hickory striker. The pencil-shaped piece of seasoned hickory, used with a glass call, had a big heavy knob on the top. As the gobbler lined up behind a big pine, Cecil flipped the striker toward Granddad. It landed softly in the pine needles to Grand-dad's left. Granddad did not stir. Cecil tried again. The next one landed to the right and a little further out – nothing. On the third try, a finely turned Red Bud striker hit the pine tree Grand-dad was sleeping against. It hit solidly just behind his head and made an uncommonly loud whap. Things began to happen very quickly at that point.

Granddad woke up with a start and instinctively began to swing his gun to the right. The turkey instinctively began to leave the county. At about forty-five yards Granddad's gun barrel caught up with the gobbler's head and a large load of No. 6s began to catch up with the turkey. The gobbler stumbled and started flopping on the ground.

Cecil was on his feet and running toward Granddad and the turkey. As Cecil approached Granddad, the turkey regained his balance and raced toward the pines on the opposite side of the power line.

As Cecil passed Granddad, Cecil grabbed the gun out of Granddad's hands and started out on the power line, firing at the old Tom. He ran out of shells as the turkey escaped into the pines, and Granddad saw Cecil lay down the gun as he footraced the turkey at a full throttle down one of those long pine runs.

The turkey stayed about fifty yards ahead for the first hundred yards, but Cecil's 200-plus pounds and short legs began to give the turkey the advantage. Cecil finally gave out and fell down in the deep pine straw as he watched the turkey streak ahead.

Cecil was breathing hard and about to give up all hope of ever seeing that monster Tom again. Then he saw the turkey break out of the pines at the end of the row, cross twenty feet of sand at the property line, and run right slap dab into a big live oak tree. Cecil realized, as the turkey flopped in the sandy soil and tried to right itself, that it had been injured by Granddad's shot, and it could not see a thing. The gobbler again got its balance and started running, this time right back toward Cecil, but four rows over from where Cecil lay watching in disbelief.

By the time Cecil got his wits about him and made it four rows over, the turkey passed at top speed. Cecil was after him with renewed hope and determination. The turkey and Cecil were heading right back toward the power line.

Granddad had now made it across the power line, picked up the empty gun and started into the pines. Still blinded, the turkey ran straight into him. Swinging the empty gun, Granddad hit the turkey across the chest sending the bird about two feet off the ground. The blow knocked the turkey flat. When the turkey got up he jumped to the next row of pines and headed back toward Cecil. While at a dead run, Cecil had broken off a large pine knot. As the turkey came by him this time, Cecil used it to whack the turkey right in the head. As the turkey flapped and flopped, Cecil grabbed him by the neck and fell into the pine needles, too exhausted to move. The twenty-one pound Tom with one-and seven-eighths-inches long curved spurs finally lay dead across Cecil's chest.

It was almost dark when those two old characters rolled into camp. Dad and I were sitting on top of the oversize picnic table outside the hunting lodge as they drove up.

I was off the table first.

I called out "How'd you do?"

The two old-timers got out of the truck, heads down, acting all defeated and put out. They were poor actors. All of us leaned over the pickup bed and looked at the biggest turkey any of us had ever killed.

Cecil winked at my granddad and, with a briar-eating smile said, "Big possums walk late."

Written for John Faris, Sr. on his ninety-first birthday, June 2006

BIGGER FISH TO FRY

Shimmering silvery moonlight rode the ripples into ever-expanding circles. The fish slowly moved forward, the top of his tail and dorsal fin now sticking out of the skinny water. He was easing closer to his target.

Scarcely ten yards away, I was sitting in a small wooden boat, fly rod across my lap, watching the drama unfold.

I had been hitting the bream beds around the shallow edges of my grandfather's seven-acre lake since half past four. It was now nine o'clock at night. Using my fiberglass L.L. Bean mail-order fly rod and a small, orange, rubber spider, I had collected thirty or so double-hand-size shellcrackers. I was quietly paddling back up the far side of the lake when the water's movement first caught my eye. The deep croaking of a lovesick bullfrog echoed from the direction of the ripples. It was almost dark. A full moon sat balanced atop the old-growth trees on the hill above the boathouse.

Another series of croaks and I was able to pick out the big, deep-voiced frog sitting on a tiny, grassy island just off the bank. The water was no more than hand deep where he sat. Old Bully was really letting it roll, broadcasting to all the females where he was and that he was more than ready for their companionship.

It was early summer and courtship filled the air. He felt safe on his private island in that very shallow water.

He was wrong. Dead wrong.

As the frog was midway into a particularly loud and long series of croaks, the bass made his move. With strong thrusts of his tail he surged through the water and mud, rapidly crossing the six-foot distance to his supper.

Mr. Bullfrog saw the impending doom, but he had not sensed the danger in time. The fish made one more mighty push of his powerful tail, and was airborne. The frog sprang from his little kingdom as the half-gallon, Mason-jar-size mouth inhaled the frog's head and the front two-thirds of his shiny, slick green body. Only the long, now helpless, hind legs protruded from the bass's mouth as he fell on muddy, but solid ground. Legs still kicking from his mouth, the bass arched his powerful body back and forth, back and forth, as he flopped toward the water. Mud went flying everywhere. Finally the huge fish, with supper deep in his throat, reached the shallow water again and righted himself. Once more the mirrored surface of the lake was broken as the bass wiggled the last few feet back into deeper water.

As I sat there and watched the moonlight catch the final ripples, I took a deep breath. Two thoughts crossed my mind. First, I had seen the largest largemouth bass I would probably ever see in my life. Second, I would spend the rest of that summer trying to catch Mr. Record Breaker.

That was Saturday. Little did I know that Sunday was to be another memorable day.

Savannah had been in our small town for two weeks when I first met her in that summer of 1959. At eighteen, she was four years older than I was. I would learn that she was much different than the girls I had grown up with and who were in my high school classes.

Savannah had arrived from Italy where she was living with her father, a colonel in the United States Army serving with the Diplomatic Corps. Savannah had been in boarding school in Paris for three years and now was to spend the entire three months of summer with her aging grandfather, Mr. Ashburn. I wondered how Savannah would take to our small Southern town with the entire population being approximately 6,000, counting every man, woman, and child.

I was quite surprised to meet her. It was on a warm, summer Sunday morning. Mr. Ashburn, Savannah's paternal grandfather, lived in an older brick house across from the First Baptist Church on West Main Street.

My mother's entire family, for several generations, had been members. The adults of my family were considered pillars of the church. In a small town Southern Baptist church, this meant from the cradle to the grave. My family and I attended services at least three times every week. Members of the family taught Sunday School classes, cooked casseroles for Wednesday night suppers, and played the piano or led the singing at prayer meetings.

As children we were not allowed to play cards, go to the picture show, or hunt on Sundays. For some unfathomable reason, however, we were allowed to go fishing on Sunday, after church of course. I always wondered if it had something to do with the majority of the deacons of the church being big fishermen, but not regular hunters.

It was my custom on most Sunday mornings to leave right after my Sunday School class was over, run across the street to Mr. Ashburn's house, and talk about fishing, both Mr. Ashburn's and my favorite subject. These weekly visits lasted about twenty minutes and then it was off to join my family in the morning worship service, which lasted until noon or longer if the preacher got really wound up.

Mr. Ashburn, who was confined to a wheelchair now, had been an avid freshwater fly fisherman through the years, and his fishing stories fascinated me. I loved those brief weekly meetings, but this warm, sunny, June Sunday morning my visit was to be different.

As I knocked on the door and started to let myself in, I almost ran over Savannah. I said, "Excuse me," and took a step back toward the door.

Just then Mr. Ashburn called from the sitting room on the east side of the house, "Johnny is that you? Come on back."

The attractive young girl who stood in the doorway stepped aside slightly, and I walked past her, went through the darkened front room, and into the bright, sunlit sitting room. It was Mr. Ashburn's favorite place.

As I entered the room, Mr. Ashburn said, "Oh! I see you've met my granddaughter already." As I looked over my shoulder I could see she had followed me into the room.

"Johnny, I want you to get to know Savannah. She is here for a while."

I awkwardly stuck out my right hand. She looked at my hand for a split second before taking it in hers. She gave me a very firm, no-nonsense handshake.

Mr. Ashburn continued, "I hope you will help me entertain Savannah this summer. I'm an old man, and she'll be bored to death hanging around here with me. Please do take her to meet some of your friends."

As her grandfather spoke, Savannah sat down on a low ottoman beside her grandfather. She was almost as tall as I was. Her long, straight hair touched the middle of her back. It was the color of polished ebony. Her skin had the look of a perpetual summer tan. There was an ever so slight oriental appearance to her high cheekbones and dark eyes. As she sat on the low footstool, she stretched her long legs out, crossed them at the ankles, and leaned back on her hands. The only thing about Savannah that remotely reminded me of any of the girls I went to Laurens High School with was her long-sleeved white blouse and faded blue jeans. She had yet to speak a word.

Mr. Ashburn and I were dyed-in-the-wool fly fishermen, an uncommon sport in the late fifties. It never became very popular in our part of South Carolina. Mr. Ashburn, my father, and I were perhaps the only three fishermen in town that I knew who used a fly rod. My dad began teaching me when I was eight years old. Six years later, with many hours on the water under my dad's tutelage, I was almost as good as he was. My dad was a very good fly fisherman.

By this time I was a true believer in fly fishing. Delicately laying the proper fly down at the end of a long, well-executed cast was the most deadly fishing technique I had ever tried.

Oh, don't misunderstand. I would quite often slip a five-inch night crawler, a green and yellow Catawba worm, or a fat cricket on a long shank hook tied to a limber Calcutta cane pole and wear out a bream bed. I was certainly happy to cast a closed face Zebco reel loaded with a ten-inch-long Black Magic pork rind to every hungry bass in the pond. I was not above hand cutting a piece of my mom's fatback into frog-shaped legs and slapping the still-smooth surface of after-dark bass haunts with a jigger pole. But given the option, fly fishing was my passion.

Mr. Ashburn and I visited a few minutes, and it didn't take long for the conversation to turn to fishing. I told him of the great bream and bluegill fishing that was still going on, but had, as usual, peaked on the full moon in May. He wanted to know what flies they had hit best and what time of day the fish were feeding.

It was not the pan fish I wanted to talk about. Instead I excitedly told him of the extraordinary largemouth bass that I had seen chasing minnows up in the shallow grass late last evening. In explicit detail I shared the exciting episode of the frog.

As I told the story, I occasionally stole a glance at Savannah. She seemed surprisingly interested. As the time came to go to church, I rose and said to Mr. Ashburn that I would see him next week.

To my utter amazement, I heard myself say, "Savannah, would you like to go fishing this afternoon?"

The first words I heard her speak that summer were, "Yes, I would."

I looked at my Timex watch and said, "I'll pick you up at three o'clock. What you have on will be fine. Long sleeves and long pants will be best if it's buggy."

I turned and let myself out.

Church seemed to last forever. Mother's fried chicken with homemade milk gravy, rice, garden fresh green beans, and creamed corn were top on my list. But the meal seemed to take an eternity to get to the table this Sunday.

At last, by two o'clock, I was packing up my five-weight fly rod, two cane poles, a small wooden tackle box that I had made in my Dad's downstairs woodworking shop, my favorite paddle, two seat cushions, the wire fish basket, and a small wire bait bucket.

Four months earlier I had gotten my permanent driver's license. I was allowed to drive the six-cylinder, black Nova station wagon, our family's backup car.

My mother was ecstatic that I now had aged up to my driver's license. I no longer had to beg her to drop me off and pick me up at remote farm ponds or lakes. Once I got my license at age fourteen, in Laurens County no fish or duck was safe. My driver's license and that little station wagon were gifts straight from heaven, of that I was sure. They were sorta payback for suffering through long, hot, summer Sunday morning worship services and weekly piano lessons.

I pulled up to 305 West Main Street at three o'clock sharp. Savannah was right on time. When I knocked on the door she appeared instantly. She was wearing the same outfit she had on that morning with the addition of short, well-worn hiking boots. She had rolled up her sleeves and tied her hair back in a long ponytail. As I had been taught by my dad, I opened the car door for her. By the time I got to my side, she had rolled down her window and pushed the vent window fully out to catch the breeze. With her arm propped on the open windowsill, she looked as if she were getting in this car and going with me for the hundredth time. I instantly felt as comfortable with this stranger as she seemed to be with me.

It was then, for the first of many times that brief summer, I noted I could tell when Savannah was near, even if I could not see her. It was like something in the air around her. She wore no perfume. There was no hint of soap or shampoo. Whatever the fragrance was, in the heat of the car that June afternoon it was totally intoxicating. Unlike the girls I had grown up knowing, with Savannah there was nothing to cause any expectation of our relationship, either short- or long-term.

It was simply a beautiful summer afternoon, and we were just going fishing!

As I started the car I asked her if she had been fishing before. She answered that her father had taught her many things, but fishing was not one of them.

"Don't worry" I said, "I'll show you how. We should catch some nice-size shellcrackers or bluegills. They're called bream around here, and they've been really hitting the crickets these last few weeks."

I turned the car around and headed out Greenwood Road to Bolt's Bait Shop. We would pass two other bait shops on the way, but Bolt's was the best place to buy fresh bait. It was built under a group of large poplar trees on a shady slope which dropped to a tumbling stream close to the back of the bait shop.

We pulled up, stopping well within the shade of the trees. I let the back window of the station wagon down, got the bait bucket out, and said, "Come on in. We'll get some crickets and something cold to drink."

The small building had that quiet, cluttered feel of all country stores. It offered just about anything you could imagine for a day on the lake. There were shelves of brightly hand-painted corks, display cards of black-and-white porcupine quill floats, and hooks in small die cut boxes either all the same size or in assortments. There were sinkers of all shapes and sizes from the smallest split shot on up. An array of various length, shellacked cane poles hung in racks from the wooden rafters. There were small glass jars of dyed pork rind in black, green, and dark purple colors. There were cardboard displays of white and yellow Shyster spinning baits. Glass-front cabinets held boxes of individual plugs like Jitter Bugs, Hawaiian Wigglers, River Runts, and Pal-O-Mine Minnows.

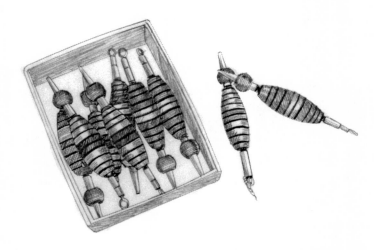

It was a place where a fisherman could spend hours.

Today, however, I only needed four dozen fresh live crickets, so I led Savannah through the small backdoor. An ad for Merita Bread was stenciled on the screen.

We stepped down into the coolness of the live bait area. Years before, Mr. Bolt had terraced the slope of the hill behind the shop down to the creek. He had hand poured concrete on each level to create a series of terraces and walkways with long, narrow concrete tanks for the minnows. Each size of minnows had their own tank. Cool water was pumped from the creek below and into the tanks through one-inch galvanized pipe with small holes. This caused the water to splash and bubble into each tank, giving the minnows extra oxygen. That made them very lively. They would be hard to catch if not for the small hand-dip nets that hung above each tank.

On the third and lowest terrace, just above the noisy little creek, was the wooden cricket cage. Inside the screen-wired cage was a small, bare light bulb. Hundreds of chirping, jumping crickets were drawn to its warmth. There was no net here, just a small glass tube graduated on the side to show the number of dozen crickets the tube held. This tube had a large red funnel that fit into its top.

We waited for Mr. Bolt. He was very particular about his live bait. He was out front pumping gas. There was no self-ser-vice. A dollar's worth of gas in those days was enough to drive to Greenwood Lake, spend the day, and drive back with plenty of gas to get to work the coming week.

When Mr. Bolt finished with his customer, he met us at the cricket cage. "Johnny," he asked, "How many you want this afternoon?"

"Four dozen will be okay today," I replied.

There was a piece of gray cardboard egg carton at one end of the cricket cage near the light. Dozens of the crickets were attracted to the carton and would climb onto it. Mr. Bolt expertly picked up that carton and tapped it on the red funnel. A hoard of crickets fell and filled the glass tube. He then held it to the light, dumped out about two inches of the insects, held it up again, and thumped the glass tube with his forefinger. After sighting the four dozen line, he tilted the tube over the cage, tapped on the

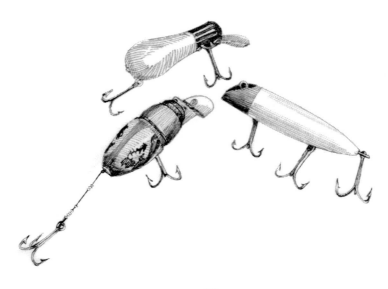

tube until two crickets fell out, and sighted one more time. He thumped the tube again with his finger and caused the crickets to settle at the appropriate four-dozen level. You would have thought Mr. Bolt and I were trading in top quality diamonds. Finally he allowed me to hold my wire bait bucket while he dumped the crickets in.

Savannah and I followed Mr. Bolt up to the cash register. I headed toward the Coca-Cola box, and asked Savannah if she wanted a Coke. She said no, but she would like a cold beer. As I turned to her I saw Mr. Bolt's head pop up and look at her from behind the cash register.

I lowered my voice whispering, "They don't sell beer here, Savannah. Besides, you can't buy beer until you're eighteen."

"I am eighteen," she said.

"Well, it's Sunday, and you can't buy beer on Sunday no matter how old you are," I explained. "They have Coca-Cola, Dr. Pepper, Orange Crush, 7-Up, and Cream Soda," I added, as we peered down at the brightly colored caps of the bottles almost submerged in a tub of ice-cold water. As she selected a six-ounce Coca-Cola, I pulled a twelve-ounce Dr. Pepper out, and picked up for us each a Moon Pie on the way to the cash register.

When we got to the counter I said to Mr. Bolt, "This is Mr. Ashburn's granddaughter, Savannah, and she's staying with her grandfather for a while. She's from Italy." I quickly added, hopefully by way of explanation.

Mr. Bolt gave Savannah an up-and-down look, a little too long, I thought. He then glanced back at me and raised one eyebrow. I shifted my gaze and studied the basket of crickets as if I had never seen any before.

As Mr. Bolt gave me my change, I looked up at him. He glanced at Savannah once more. Raising that eyebrow again, he said, "Good luck."

My granddad's farm was on the Yarborough Mill Road. By the time we had finished off the sodas and Moon Pies, I was pulling the little black station wagon up to the white, wooden gate. The dirt road beyond led to the lake. I got out, unlocked the chained gate, drove through, stopped just inside, got out, and carefully closed the gate.

Granddad raised registered whiteface Hereford cows, and it wouldn't do for them to be scattered all over Yarborough Mill Road. That lesson had been hard learned last summer when I had not latched the gate properly.

I was with my dad that trip. He was driving. In the country it is proper etiquette for the youngest in the pickup truck or car to get out and open and close the gate. No young person, girl or boy, raised in the country, would ever think of sitting still as the vehicle approached a closed gate. They would immediately hop out to undo the gate and then close it back.

I remembered that particular day. After my dad drove through the gate, I closed it. In my haste I did not latch it back well. After Dad slowly eased the car through the herd of big cows congregated near the gate, they must have bumped it. While we were fishing that evening, the gate swung open. At nine o'clock that night Dad and I were still trying to round up thirty-four prize Herefords off the tar-and-gravel road and back into the pasture.

Dad and I agreed never to tell my grandfather.

It was a short downhill drive past the big barn, past the tall, hand-laid rock silo, through the virgin stand of red and white

oaks to the ridge overlooking one of the most beautiful and productive man-made lakes I have ever known.

I was only a young boy when the lake was built, but I could
recall much of the planning and construction. Before the dam
was begun, a swift, bold stream wound its way through a long,
heavily wooded narrow valley. My dad often took me out on
Sunday afternoons to see the progress as the lake took shape.

First, all the trees had to be cut and burned. The two-foot-
wide corrugated drain pipe was laid in a bed of red clay right
where the creek bed was. The dam was then built wide enough
to drive a farm tractor across. For a small boy it was fascinating
to watch the lake being constructed and to see the water slowly
beginning to fill it. One month, two, three, then four, and still
there was much area to be filled.

It was at about the fifth month when Granddad had the post
and pilings set for the two boathouses and the fishing dock. It
was also about this time, with the water still eight to ten feet from
filling the lake, that my dad and I would walk along the rising
water's edge. Dad let me guess where I thought the water would
finally come as we looked at the remaining trees, newly-cut
stumps, flat grassy meadows, and steep rocky ridges. We tried to
envision and imprint in our minds for all time, what these last few
feet of shore would look like once covered by water forever. Old
intersecting gullies would be transformed into inviting coves,
grassy meadows would become shallow fish-feeding flats, and
steep ridges would become cool, deep lunker hideouts in the late
summer heat.

The time spent watching the lake fill made an impression on
me. Through the years there were few, if any, good fishing spots
there that I didn't know like the back of my hand.

As I pulled the car to a stop overlooking the boat houses and dock I knew exactly where I would take Savannah this afternoon for her first fishing lesson. About sixty feet to the left of an old stump, directly across the lake from the dock, was a spreading beech tree. The tree's lower branches touched the water in a semicircle fashion, protecting a large area of shady, shallow water. The tree's size suggested it was pushing its one-hundredth birthday.

At this time of year the shellcrackers and bluegills had fanned out four dozen or so beds in which their eggs had been laid and fertilized. These beds resembled foot-wide white saucers in the dark, thin water. These nurseries were jealously guarded by both parents. Any bug approaching within several feet of home was immediately engulfed by either Mom or Pop. It was here that Savannah would learn to catch fish.

I unloaded the gear, and handed Savannah the paddle, boat cushions, and fish basket. After gathering up the rods, bait, and tackle box, I led her down the brick walk and into the wide, wooden, low-ceilinged boat house. This was where my Uncle Jim kept an aluminum boat fitted with a five-horsepower Evinrude outboard motor. No one but my uncle ever used this boat. He liked to troll for bass and never fished any other way.

Dad, Granddad and I never trolled so there was a separate and much smaller covered area for our long, slender, handmade wooden paddle boat. It was painted porch green in color. A wonderful fishing boat, it was twelve feet long, quite narrow for its length, and it had a comfortable seat at either end. Best of all, It was very easy to paddle.

I unlocked the boat, pulled the rusty chain through the sheer, and slid the slender craft out from under its cover parallel to the low board walkway. In went the gear, and we were off in the direction of the old beech tree.

I pushed from the dock and took a couple of strokes toward our destination with the paddle. I put it across the gunwales and just let the boat drift into the middle of the flat, calm lake.

Class was now in session. I picked up the lighter and shorter of the two cane poles, and pulled the long, thin hook from the butt end where it had been stuck in the soft bamboo for safe transport. Then I rolled the pole over and over to unwind the six-pound-test monofilament line. Finally I slipped the red wooden peg from the top of the worn yellow cork and slid the cork to twelve inches above the hook. Savannah watched all this in silence.

When I had the pole all ready I said, "Here's how it works, Savannah. We're going over there toward that large beech tree with its branches in the water." With the pole I pointed toward the towering beech tree and asked, "See how the fish are moving the water under the limbs?"

"No," she answered, "I don't see where you are talking about."

"Look now, see that giant stump in the water? It's the biggest tree just to the left. See the limbs touching the water? Watch closely, and look just inside the limbs. You'll see the fish roil the water."

I pointed again, and we sat there a few moments. A big bream smacked a bug that had the misfortune of falling from the limb above. Several other fish swirled in anticipation.

"Oh! I see them now. I see them!" she said with much excitement.

"Good, now let me show you what you have to do."

I plucked a big, fat, lively cricket from the wire bait basket and threaded it onto the hook. I started the thin hook right below its head, down the length of its body, and out the rear. The cricket spat what we called tobacco juice at me as I adjusted it so that it sat perfectly and naturally on the hook. I held the line right above the hook in my left hand and the pole in my right.

"Give the pole just a gentle swinging motion, let the line go, and drop the cricket in the water wherever you want it to go."

I demonstrated. The cricket swung out and gently dropped at the end on the ten-foot line.

"Watch the cork. See how it follows the cricket? As the cricket sinks, the float follows along. When it is at the full twelve-inch depth see how the cork tips up? The fish often will hit the bait while the cricket is drifting down, so watch the cork carefully. It'll start moving faster than normal and then suddenly disappear. That's when you want to gently pull back to set the hook. Don't pull or jerk back hard. Just gently." I emphasized.

"The water's very shallow in there, so when you get one on I'm going to backpaddle. You just lead the fish out so we don't spook the rest of them. We want to catch several out of that area. When we get back away from the bream bed some, you can lead the fish over to my end of the boat, and I'll take it off and put another cricket on. Then we'll see if we can get another one."

"Think you got it?" I asked.

"I think so. Let me try," she said.

I handed her the pole and said, "Let's practice a couple of times out here in the deeper water."

Savannah took the limber pole and tried to catch the line. It swung past her, once on the left side. Then it swung once to the right, closely passing my head, and back out front. With one long reach she finally caught the line. She smiled at me in apology.

I said, "It's okay, you're doing fine. Now hold the line right above the hook and swing it out. Let go of the hook."

After three or four jerky attempts and noisy plops of the hook and cork, she began to get the feel of it.

I finally said, "That's pretty good. Let's give 'em a try. You get ready but don't go until I stop the boat and tell you when," I said.

I eased the boat forward. When I was twenty-five feet away from the closest limb, I swung the boat parallel to the bank and backpaddled once. The boat came to a gentle stop.

"Savannah, aim for the closest limb. Just ease it in there. Try not to hit a branch."

She was pretty well coordinated, and the first attempt was good, but a little short.

I said, "That's fine. Let it sit there."

I knew the hook was probably a little too far out, but that was better for the first attempt than being too far in. Savannah might get the hook hung up and spook the whole school of fish. The little, yellow cork sat a full two minutes before I told her to pick it up and try a little closer.

She did just as I told her. This time the cricket touched down within a hand's width of where the leafy twig touched the water. Instantly we saw a large swirl, and the two-inch-long yellow cork disappeared below the surface like it had been fired from a gun. Savannah's instinct took over, and she hauled back with all her strength. The big broad fish dashed under the tree, and the pole almost went double. The line cut through the water with a singing sound. As the fish got closer to the surface, it lost its advantage. Then Savannah and the limber pole won out.

The pound-size, dark purple-and-orange oval shot out from under the tree, became airborne, passed Savannah's head as she screamed, and passed my head as I ducked. It got to the

80

end of the line some ten feet behind the boat and started back toward us. I ducked a second time, but Savannah wasn't quick enough. The broad, flat side of the fish hit her right in the forehead, nearly knocking her backward into the water. The fish slid full length down her face, down the front of her white blouse, into her lap, and finally ended up flapping around the floor of the boat. Savannah dropped to her knees, grabbed the fish in both hands, and held her prize up as she whooped and hollered.

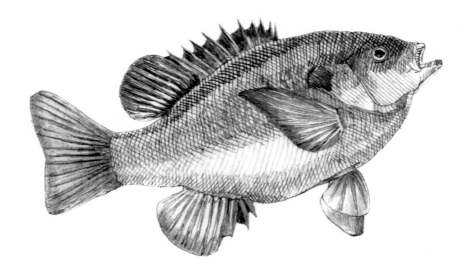

I was laughing so hard I was not much help. At last I retrieved her trophy, gently extracted the hook, held it up one last time for her approval, and dropped it into the fish basket I had tied to the boat's right side. As I retrieved the pole and hook and rebaited it, Savannah leaned over the side of the boat, scooped a great double-handful of pond water and splashed it over her face. As the water dripped from her cheeks and nose, she leaned over once more to wash her hands in the lake. She pulled her shirttail out of her tight-fitting jeans and used it to wipe her face while exposing a lot of trim, tanned midriff. It was quite clear she was wearing nothing beneath her now soaking wet, white cotton blouse. I couldn't resist smiling, and she caught me in the act.

She glanced down at the front of her blouse, realized the cause of my reaction, and asked "What are you smiling so about?"

"Uh, uh, nice blouse," I stammered. I was concentrating as hard as I could on grabbing another cricket out of the bait bucket.

I thought, *What in the world are you saying?*

In an attempt to change the subject I suggested, "Let's see if we can catch another one. But, don't jerk so hard this time. Just ease back on the line when the cork goes under. Try to keep 'em in the water."

Savannah was a quick learner and had excellent eye-hand coordination. She caught seven more really nice shellcrackers before she got a little too excited and wrapped two feet of line around one of the lower twigs. She jerked the pole back to free the line and moved the limb considerably in doing so. The water under the tree boiled as two dozen or more healthy bream spooked and headed for deeper water.

"No, no, don't pull!" I loudly whispered. "Don't spook them! Lay your pole in the water, and leave it there. It'll just float there."

She reluctantly did as I told her. I pulled back on the paddle, moving the boat twenty feet or so away from the tree. The pole floated in the water with the line tangled around the limb.

"We'll let them rest a minute," I explained. "We'll get the pole and untangle the line last thing."

As we waited for the fish to settle down, I picked up the fly rod, tied on a bright orange, foam rubber spider with six white rubber legs. I stripped forty feet of line from the reel and placed it in the bottom of the boat.

I said to her "We spooked them pretty good. The water's very shallow in there. We'll ease back up, and I'll see if I can pull a couple more out on a fly. We'll stay out further, and they may settle down."

I laid the fly rod across the gunwale, let ten feet of line and the saucy little spider trail in the water, picked up the paddle, and moved the boat so I could cast to the far left side of the bream bed. As I moved the boat, a slight breeze drifted toward us with the distinct smell of watermelon.

"Smell that?" I asked.

"What?" she said.

"Take a deep breath and tell me what you smell," I said.

She breathed in. "I don't know. It's sort of a sweet, musky smell. What is it?"

"Does it smell like watermelon to you?" I asked.

"Yes, yes, it does! What does it come from?"

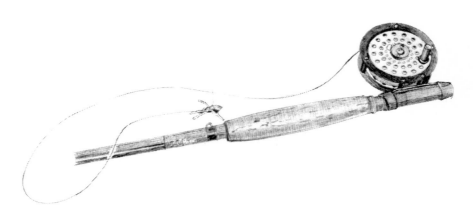

83

"It's the shellcrackers and bluegills. Whenever you smell that you know you are very close to their bed, usually a very large group of them. Sometimes it's the quickest way to find them when they are in deeper water."

The boat was now fifty feet from the magic spot. I brought it to a stop, put down the paddle and picked up the well-used fly rod in my right hand and the coils of extra line in my left. After three false casts I let just enough slide through the fingers on my left hand to allow the end of the light yellow floating section to settle six feet from the outside tree limb. As the six-foot leader laid a soft loop out, it passed narrowly between two twigs, and the orange foam spider settled ten inches inside the dark shadows. I let it lie perfectly still while the small concentric circles moved out and away. I waited a slow count to ten and then barely twitched the rod tip. The spider lightly danced on its rubber legs then disappeared in a mini-explosion. I pulled my left hand back, setting the hook as the big female shellcracker headed in the opposite direction.

"Holy cow!" Savannah cried.

I took the line in my right hand and held tight against the stained cork grip of the rod. A large bow in the rod kept the line tight. I grabbed the paddle with my left hand so that I could pull the boat and fish away from the tree and the rest of the school. I played the big bream and enjoyed feeling the line cut through the warm summer water. Two minutes later I lifted the biggest shellcracker of the day over the shallow gunwale. It was so broad I couldn't get my hands around it, so I pinned it to the boat bottom with one hand and slid the hook out of its lip with the other. I held the fish up, and we both admired its glistening golds, greens, and blacks in the strong late afternoon light. It was one of the biggest of the season and must have weighed twice as much as any that Savannah had caught.

"Holy cow!" Savannah said again. "That was beautiful! What a fish! I want to learn how to catch them with a fly rod. Will you show me how to use one of those?"

"Sure, we'll practice. You can learn to cast a fly rod. No problem." I promised. "It's getting late though. Watch me, and I'll try to catch a couple more right quick. That'll give you and your granddad enough for a meal."

I repeated the performance twice more, and we were back at the dock as dusk settled over the narrow valley. As I was cleaning the ten fat bream for the frying pan, we heard a huge splash and both looked up in time to see a very large fish boiling the shallow water behind the big stump. For a full five minutes that monster plowed through the grass with a third of its wide back out of the water, stirring up mud with its strong tail and scattering half-grown bream in all directions. From all the way across the lake I knew it had to be him, the same giant bass I had seen the night before.

Even to Savannah's inexperienced eye, the big fish was impressive.

"Holy cow!" she said for the third time that day. "Johnny, let's catch that one."

"No, no, not tonight," I said, knowing full well that nobody was going to be casting to that fish but me. That one was to be all mine. Besides I thought it was going to be hard as heck to get that old boy to bite. The spot he was feeding in was almost impossible to reach without spooking such a big experienced fish.

As I finished scaling and gutting the bream, the old lunker made one more lunge through the shallows. We could only hear him now. It was too dark to see him glide back into the three feet of dark, cool water right behind the big oak stump. Savannah stood and rinsed off the fish in the lake water as I handed them to her and dropped the dripping, now scaleless, cleaned fish back into the wire basket.

She stood up, wiped her hands on the legs of her jeans and said, "That was so much fun. Thanks for bringing me."

"I enjoyed it too," I said. "You did really well. Your grandfather's going to be very impressed," I said as I held up the basket. "It's pretty late. Let's get you back to town."

We divided up the gear. Savannah wanted to carry the fish, so we added them to her half of the equipment and headed up the steep walk. I started the car and turned on the lights so we could see. I lowered the station wagon's tailgate. I spread out several sheets of the weekend newspaper to set the fish on and slid the fly rod and cane poles over the backseat and front seat, resting the butt ends on the dashboard.

As we went to get in, I noticed a huge spider web caught in the beam of the headlights. Seeing such a big, fresh web formed at this time of night meant beautiful fair weather the next day. I could not resist.

"Come around the front of the car, and let me show you something," I told Savannah.

As she came around I led her to the large, symmetrical web, making her stand to one side so the light from the car beams would not be blocked.

"When you see a new web like that you know it's going to be a good fishing day the next day. The spider knows not to go to all that hard work if the rain and wind are coming," I said.

"It's beautiful. I've never seen one so perfect," she said.

I pointed to the upper left-hand section, almost two feet from the tightly woven center and almost out of the light. There was the master builder and hunter. Almost two inches of black and yellow, its body was as large as the end of my little finger.

"Watch this." I grabbed the first big moth that passed in front of the bright beams and threw the fluttering creature against the center of the web. The instant the moth touched the web the hungry spider raced down the silky strands and covered the moth with more sticky silk threads. The moth stopped moving in seconds.

"Holy cow," Savannah whispered.

We retraced our path back up to the gate, careful to unlock and relock it, and I had her home by ten o'clock. I sent her inside to get a big bowl. When she returned, I pushed open the spring-loaded bottom of the wire fish basket and let her first mess of fish slide into the bowl. She looked down at the full bowl in the light of the single bulb hanging above the porch, then up at me.

"Thank you, I had a wonderful time," she said. She slipped her right hand behind my neck, pulled me toward her slightly, and kissed me. This was not a peck on the cheek by my Aunt Laura. I thought I was never going to get to breathe again. For the first time in my life, here I was being kissed by a very beautiful girl, and I had met her only eleven hours before.

Holy cow!

As she stepped back slightly, I finally remembered to breathe, and I blurted out "You wanna practice that some more tomorrow?"

Savannah laughed out loud.

I stammered, "No, I mean would you like to go practice fishing some more tomorrow?"

She answered, "That sounds like great fun!" She then cocked her head slightly, smiled, and said "Yes, let's do try that some more tomorrow."

On the short drive home, the warm summer night flooded through the open windows. The tingle of my first real kiss held a big smile on my face. My thought was, *Yes, sir, there's the record-breaking bass to catch, but this summer there may be bigger fish to fry.*

THE BRIDGE AT LITTLE MOUNTAIN

The chopper was close, very close, and coming fast. The noise was building quickly to a deafening and familiar whop-whop-whop. The helicopter had to be flying quite low. Even though it sounded so close, I could not see it yet. I knew when the chopper popped over the trees it would be right on top of me. I would have to shoot very quickly and be right on target.

My gun was almost at my shoulder as I glanced from the top of the tree line to the green watery tunnel. They were coming. I knocked off the safety as my gun came up.

I never heard the first shot.

But I'm getting a little ahead of myself.

Early in November with the beginning of duck season only two Saturdays away, Sammy and I stayed busy, trying to pin down as many good duck hunting spots as possible. Sammy was my fourteen-year-old, regular duck hunting partner. He was a year younger than I was. We had been hunting together for five years.

The ducks in our part of the county, in the upper Piedmont of South Carolina, would locate a good stretch of water with ample food. They would return from roosting each night to that exact locale, day after day, until the food gave out or the hunting pressure became too great. Once Sammy and I located a good group of ducks, we shot there no more than once a week. We didn't want to run them off.

I don't know how other folks located ducks, but Sammy and I had been taught by the master, Sammy's granddad. He was the dean of duck hunting and had probably killed more ducks than anyone else in our area. The system we learned from him and used so successfully took at least two people, many hours, and lots of walking.

Our timeworn method worked this way.

Sammy and I, by age fourteen, knew where every bridge in three counties crossed any kind of sizeable creek or river. The Reedy River and Rabon Creek were our two most productive tributaries.

Sammy and I patiently worked one river or creek at a time. Since all the rivers and creeks in our area flowed into Greenwood Lake, we began as close to this lake as possible. It was there that all the big ducks roosted each evening. The ducks would leave the lake before daylight. They flew up the various creeks and rivers to the closest good, big sandbar with water oak acorn trees growing over or nearby. The ducks would land there between 6:45 and 7:00 A.M. Their punctual arrival was only slightly altered by the amount of sunshine. A cloudy day might add fifteen-to-twenty minutes to their arrival time.

About thirty minutes before dark in the evenings, I let Sammy out at the first bridge, and then I drove around to the next bridge upriver located a mile or two away. All the ducks would fly back down the river to Greenwood Lake just before dark. I counted the ducks that passed over me as long as I could see them in the waning light. Then I drove back down the river to pick up Sammy.

As we drove home, we compared numbers. If Sammy saw ducks that I didn't, then you could bet they were feeding somewhere between the two bridges. If I saw ducks and Sammy did also, we knew they were feeding further upriver from me. The next evening I would drop Sammy off at my bridge and then drive one bridge farther up to see if any ducks flew over it.

We repeated the process until we had the ducks bracketed. Then the investigation took some serious legwork. Not all the enticing food sources were directly on the river or creek proper. Most of the time they were, but sometimes it was a swamp off the river.

Before duck season opened, most Saturdays would find us walking from one bridge to the next, carefully searching for the ducks' feeding area. Once we found it, we tried not to run them out but quietly waited until they flew out naturally at nightfall. We would brush up a tree or two to use for cover at a later time. Then, marking the path in our minds as best we could, we made our way back to the car. We knew we would have to return this way in the pitch of dark some morning several weeks hence.

It was on one of these evening reconnaissance missions that Sammy and I stumbled upon a most unusual place where we found hundreds of black ducks. They were in a location where Sammy's granddad had never hunted ducks before. You would have had to know Sammy's granddad to understand what a rare find this was. Sammy and I were very excited and pleased with ourselves.

The new place we had come across was farther upriver from the lake than we had ever been. The night before, we had seen well over a hundred large black ducks cross both bridges. A hundred ducks was a big number, and we knew we were on to something.

The following day after school we drove to the next bridge to let Sammy out. The creek was so small we just knew the ducks had to be somewhere below where we now were and the bridge I was on last evening. So we both went back down to the same bridge I had been on the night before. Sure enough, about fifteen minutes before dark, we counted well over a hundred ducks silhouetted against a very cold, winter, copper-rose sunset.

The white patch under their wings told us they were blacks.

The ducks were flying very low, all clumped in little groups of ten, fifteen, and twenty, and no more than several minutes apart. We knew that they had not come from too far upriver and were most likely all feeding together. That was on Thursday, December 17. Saturday would find the two of us on this bridge at first light.

Saturday morning the two of us were standing on a tar-and-gravel road at the end of the bridge. We parked our hunting vehicle, my family's little black Nova station wagon, on a dirt road not far from where we were standing. We purposely positioned it so it could not be seen from passing pickup trucks. There would not be many because this was a very rural part of Laurens County, but there was no use telegraphing the position of a potential new duck hunting spot to the chance passing hunter.

Sammy and I both wore hip boots. They were cuffed down to our knees and snapped there to hold them at that height until needed in potentially deeper water. We had layered on thick pants, heavy tee shirts covered by long-sleeved sweatshirts, and topped off with heavy canvas coats to protect us from the cold and briars.

At our age, every trip along the rivers or creeks was a grand adventure and was treated by the two of us as something of a survival exercise. We carried waterproof matches, sharp pocket knives, and an abundant supply of Mr. Goodbars, strictly for energy, of course. Sammy's granddad once told my dad not to worry about us. If we ever got lost all he would have to do was follow the steady trail of Mr. Goodbar candy wrappers.

As usual, this morning our pockets were full of No. 4 high brass Peter's shotgun shells for our 12-gauge guns. Sammy shot an old 12-gauge pump, and I had been shooting a Browning 12-gauge automatic since Santa Claus brought it to me when I was twelve years old. We may not have been the two best shots in the county, but we almost never missed getting our limit of doves, ducks, or rabbits.

At 6:45 A.M. six groups of black ducks came over the little bridge. They flew even lower than they had the night before, and they were talking up a storm to each other. They sounded excited as they discussed breakfast. As the last group passed, Sammy and I looked at each other in the false dawn light. We both smiled. It was clear those big boys weren't going far.

It was time to start walking. We eased off the bridge, down to the water's edge, and began to slip as quietly as possible up the little creek. When I say little, I mean very little. The creek was no wider than six feet in the curves and as narrow as three feet in the straightaway. When the going got tough on one bank, we hopped over to the opposite side and continued up the stream.

As we moved up, the creek grew ever smaller. We both started to wonder how all those ducks could be using a place like this. The edges of the creek were pretty steep, the brush thick, and there were no acorn trees. It just did not add up. Ducks like open places to land, with shallow banks and sandbars on which to feed. There they loafed in the sunshine. They must have food. Lots of acorns were their favorite.

After about a mile the land began to slope up on the right-hand bank. A short distance further it rose even more steeply. It became a small mountain, and the creek turned abruptly to the left, away from this unforeseen geological feature.

Staying with the creek we turned left. Then it happened. We took a few more soft, quiet steps and broke out into a wide-open swamp. We looked at each other in amazement. Just as we did, we heard the first soft feeding chuckles of the ducks. They were not far away.

The swamp was not like any other we had ever seen. Usually a swamp would be in very flat land. The main water source, creek or river, would get to this area and break apart, spreading itself all through the lowland like the fingers of a hand. Small ponds, potholes, and tiny tributaries connected the fingers. Button bushes and small willow trees usually grow in the most shallow parts, and on the little islands.

This one was very different. There was a little mountain on one side. The creek ran right up to its base. The land was so steep it would have been very hard to climb the first hundred feet or so. The small creek then turned out from the sharply rising ground and formed a big loop before coming back toward the mountain on the lower end of the watery woods. It was full of tall, straight pin oaks. The water was still and the bottom pretty hard.

Acorns lay everywhere. You could see the little dark balls with their orange tops and bottoms of sharp pins in the clear two-foot-deep water. We could hear the acorns falling into the quiet water like a slow rain.

Plop ....

Plop ....

Plop .... Plop

94

Whenever we heard an acorn drop, we could hear the splashing of several ducks scurrying across the surface of the water, racing each other for the prize.

We could not see the ducks yet, but we knew they were close.

Sammy and I eased up behind a big, wide poplar tree. As soon as I was behind the tree I began to unplug my gun. Most shotguns were manufactured to hold five shells. It was a federal restriction when hunting migratory birds, such as ducks, to use a gun that holds only three rounds. A plug was a wooden dowel that took up enough room in the gun's magazine to restrict it to only two shells. The two shells in the magazine, and one in the chamber made the allowable three. Unscrewing the cap on my gun and careful not to drop it in the water, I pulled the plug out, dropped the plug, a No. 2 pencil in this case, into my shirt pocket, and replaced the cap. I then pulled the barrel down as I held the butt of the stock against my thigh. I tightened the cap extra tight and as quietly as possible. I slipped two additional dark blue, high brass magnums into the chamber.

Sammy had left the bridge with his gun unplugged. Since this was not the most legal thing to do, I had always thought it best to make the change away from the road. Game wardens were not known for tough, long walks in thick brush. A fourteen-year-old could walk most wardens into the ground and, unless you were a really bad actor, almost never were you accosted by anyone.

Sammy and I had hunted for five years together, and we knew exactly what the other would do next.

I stayed fairly close to the creek; Sammy stayed as low as possible for his 6-foot-2-inch frame and moved straight toward the mountain. When he got fifty yards from me, we would stay exactly opposite each other. Neither moved ahead so as not to get into the other person's line of fire. At some point, one or both of us would spook the ducks, and a few would flush.

The cardinal rule in duck hunting is to never, ever, wait on the next person to shoot first. If you get a clean shot, you need to take it, because neither you, nor your partner, are guaranteed a second chance.

From experience, we both knew what the ducks were about to do, and we were ready. One of us would bump a small portion of the big flock. They would wildly flush. The person closest would shoot. In the confusion, the other ducks would leave the water and scramble for altitude. But they would not all flush at the same time and not all in the same direction.

We knew that over the water the sound would echo off the trees and the mountain. Some of the ducks would mistakenly flush in the wrong direction and actually fly toward us. It would all be over in a couple of minutes, but there was a good chance we would each get three or more good shots. There would not normally be time to reload, thus the reason for the unplugged magazine and the five shells.

Sammy had successfully slipped to his spot, and looking over toward me, he turned up the swamp. I pulled up my hip boots and slowly moved forward. I was bent over almost touching the water, looking hard to try to spot the ducks before they saw me.

The closer the better. The light was soft. There was a slight overcast. The entire swamp was colored in black, soft grays, and dark pewter. The dusky, dark-black ducks would be extremely well camouflaged. Movement would be their giveaway and ours too.

I pulled up behind a century-old, unusually large oak and slowly stood up. Just at that moment two ducks swam from behind the other side of the tree. The ducks were not three yards away. We saw each other at the same instant. As I raised my gun, the ducks exploded ten feet straight up in the air. I shot the right one immediately. I swung on the second and pulled the trigger. Nothing happened. I looked at the gun. The first spent shell was sticking out sideways in the receiver. Without lowering the gun I pulled the ejector hard. The shell fell away, allowing the receiver to close on the next shell. My second shot caught up with the duck at treetop level, and he folded. I was subconsciously aware that Sammy was steady after them. I turned in time to see a group of four rising from his left, heading straight for me. I missed the closest duck but got lucky when the rest of the bunch flared. One more fell clean.

Ducks were getting up everywhere now, headed out of harm's way. I saw Sammy kill a single, and then it was quiet for a minute. The entire drove of ducks banked out over the creek and headed back toward the swamp, which seems illogical but is very common. They passed over pretty high, but I caught one more with a long lead to make my fourth. I could hear Sammy reloading, and I did the same.

We waited a full five minutes to see if any more would flush. Sometimes a few of the very smart ones would sit tight through all the commotion and then slip out when you least expected it. These were the older, wiser birds. None did, so we waded out to pick up the downed birds. Sammy shot a cripple as it tried to dive under water and hide. Then all was quiet. In a few minutes we met back at the big poplar where we had split up. Sammy had matched my four with four of his own.

Even though we had just made a terrible racket shooting five times each, and there was most likely not a duck within a mile now, we continued to whisper to each other. No real hunter ever does anything but whisper after leaving the road. It's an absolute one hundred percent sure indicator of how long a person has really hunted. We were very excited by the fast action. Our adrenaline level was sky-high as we quietly, but rapidly, shared details of our individual shots and misses and marveled in hushed tones at the sheer number of big ducks.

We waded slowly back out of the swamp and then made good time back to the car. We stopped along the creek, still several hundred yards from the road and plugged both guns. We walked a little further, and I left one of my ducks with Sammy. I carried my limit of three on to the car as Sammy waited a safe distance up river. Finding no game warden at the car, I whistled twice. Sammy came out with the rest of the ducks.

Then it was off to Todd's Country Store where they made the best hot dogs in the county. Three hot dogs and a big soft drink apiece later, it was on to Sammy's granddad's house to clean the ducks.

Sammy's granddad was waiting for us. He had gone to Burton's Pond, his most favorite place, and had killed three plump, acorn-fattened mallards. They were already dressed, soaking in a big ceramic bowl of salt water with a tablespoonful of baking soda. Baking soda and salt was supposed to draw the blood out and tame their wonderful wild taste down to just the right level. The formula seemed to work, and we all cleaned, dressed, and soaked our birds the same way.

Sammy and I were very proud of ourselves. We had discovered a large group of big ducks. We found them in a brand-new place, and killed four ducks apiece, an excellent day in any duck hunter's book. As we told our story to Sammy's granddaddy, we dressed the ducks. We had a lot of duck-cleaning experience, and we had the process down to a science. Long before either of us

was old enough to carry a gun, we were allowed to go hunting with our dads, uncles, or granddads. That also meant we most likely picked up the downed ducks as long as the water was not too deep or fast, and it most definitely meant we picked and cleaned them when we returned home.

Picking up the ducks in the water got pretty interesting after mid-October. For years we never knew what a retriever was. No one had a dog like that or thought of getting one. If you shot a duck down and it fell in the water or across the water, one designated person, usually the youngest member of the hunting party stripped off their clothes and waded out to get the dead duck. It wasn't too bad until freezing weather, and then some real record-fetching times were set.

Compared to playing retriever, cleaning the ducks was a snap unless you happened to get stuck with cleaning a big pile of them by yourself. As long as there was at least one other person to help, you could rehash the entire hunt from every aspect while you worked. Then the time flew by. Sammy and I had a system, and we worked well as a team.

First we would pick all the feathers off the back, breast, and legs down to the knee joint of each bird. Then, using a sharp kindling axe, one of us would pull the wings as far out from the duck's body as possible, and the other person, expertly using the sharp little axe, would cut the wing off as close as possible to the duck's body. You really needed to trust the person using the axe, if you were the one holding the wings. After both wings were cut off all the birds, we built a small fire of newspaper on the ground and, holding the duck by the legs and head, we singed off the down and small hairs that were left. We rotated the bird rapidly over the little flames and the fat birds would be clean as a pin in seconds.

After the legs and head had served as handles for this part of the process, we used the little axe again to cut off the legs below the drumstick and the neck, as close as practical to the duck body. Finally, we split the duck down the back, cleaned out all the inside stuff, washed off the blood, and put the clean, plump birds in the big soaking bowl. We could easily do a limit of birds for four people in thirty-five minutes.

While we were carrying out this precise ritual on the eight birds lined up on the old porcelain outside cleaning sink, we told Sammy's granddad the entire story. We recounted how we found a special spot, how we carried out this morning's hunt, and the great shots we made. We failed to mention the misses. Sammy's granddad was very impressed with all this information. Big ducks, mallards, and blacks, were much prized, and a drove of one hundred was very unusual. It was planned that the whole group, Sammy's granddad, Uncle Bud, my dad, Sammy, and I would return as soon as possible to Little Mountain, as we had started calling the secret place.

The next trip to Little Mountain was a great success. Several more very productive Saturdays followed. It was such a hot spot we all agreed no one or even two of us would go and hunt there without the entire group. It would be a shame to pressure this big group of ducks with only two hunters.

There were afternoons after school when for one reason or another Sammy might not be able to hunt. Those days I was left to explore on my own. Since I would not dare go to Little Mountain alone, I decided to begin at the same bridge, park in the same out-of-sight spot on the old logging road, but hunt in the opposite direction. It would be an adventure.

You never knew what you would find when out hunting. Monday was one of those days. With a healthy pocketful of shells, I crossed the single-lane tar-and-gravel road, dropped down to the creek bank below the wooden bridge, and began exploring the bottoms.

The little creek wound through an overgrown pasture and entered the hardwoods two hundred yards below the bridge. At this point it had nice, clean, sandy banks that were not very high above the clear, slowly running water. As I walked there were more and more pin oak trees in this direction, and the place just began to look and feel ducky.

It's like that when hunting, and fishing, for that matter. Whatever game you are hunting, your successes all seem to be associated with a certain geography, cover types, or food sources. After so many years afield, you see new places and your subconscious compares the look to those stored in your mental library.

Pretty soon your mind registers, *Oh, I've seen this type place before and it was a jam-up hunting spot.*

You see a wide, flat field in late September with corn stubble and you think, *This field looks, feels, and smells like a dove field.*

You get out of a pickup truck on an old farm road, look at the old overgrown fence rows running alongside acres of knee-high golden broomstraw, and you just know you could shoot some quail there. The place was birdy, as the saying goes.

Or you walk very quietly along a creek, look up at the next bend in the creek, see the leaves still clinging to a big pin oak, and think, *This place really looks ducky.*

Duck food was everywhere. I was very encouraged. I slowed down and watched more carefully where I put my feet.

You had to keep reminding yourself. Movement and noise is what tips your hand.

If ducks were up ahead, I needed to be very quiet.

Step on a sandy spot, miss the leaves, and don't break a twig or stick.

Walk up the creek in the water if the bank gets too grown up so as to make little noise.

Be very patient, slow down.

Slow down.

Soon I could see the little creek was leading out of the timber and into the open. I was even more on guard. I eased forward, stopping often to listen to the woods. There it was, the sound of the soft, playful splashing of summer ducks. Big ducks feed, but never play. Summer ducks, or wood ducks as they are called, are very much like young children. They spend hours playing and chasing each other, making quite a racket.

There it was again, not too far up ahead. It was unmistakable. The brilliant males were noisily chasing each other away from a prize morsel. Then they came back together in a small group to feed on the acorns.

I reached into my right-hand jacket pocket and pulled out two more No. 4 12-gauge shells. I was too close to pull the plug out of my gun, so I put one shell between the first and second finger of my left hand and one between my second and third finger.

When I flushed the ducks I might need more shells in a hurry. Having these two held directly below the gun's forearm would expedite loading them.

With the gun halfway to my shoulder, I shifted my eyes constantly left to right and back again, trying to see the little ducks before they saw me. I was crouched low, taking baby steps, feeling with my front foot for a solid spot before shifting my weight forward. One step, then two. On the third one all heck broke loose.

Two dozen wood ducks flushed from between the marshy clumps of grass and water and began to climb for safety. I picked out a big drake, covered him with the barrel of my gun, raised it a foot higher, and dropped the first shot clean. The second shot was on target. Number three was a clean miss.

Never taking my eyes off the ducks, I loaded the other two shells in the gun. As the receiver slammed shut on the first shell, the ducks were making a sharp curve to the right, spreading into a single file. They were just crossing over an old rusty barbed wire fence thirty-five yards out when I dropped another drake. I was about to shoot the last shell when to my great surprise the last three ducks in the string dove into a deep-sided drainage ditch just across the barbed wire fence. It was covered over with big, heavy briars, making a tunnel over the water-filled ditch. The three ducks swam up into this sanctuary. I put two more shells in the gun as quietly as possible.

Without moving I glanced over the swamp. I could see all three dead ducks, belly-up and not moving. Assured that they would be there to pick up later, I started very slowly toward the ditch. After taking no more than five steps, I could see why these ducks had chosen this spot for escape.

The ditch was quite deep, sides straight, and the cover was very dense. Except for the entrance where the ducks dove in, there appeared to be no means of escape. There was no way to shoot these ducks without a second person. That second hunter would have to ease around to the other end and make enough noise to scare the ducks back out the way they had entered. If I went around to the rear to drive them out, they would flush out the front and be too far away for me to get a good clean kill. I was about to give it up.

I glanced back over my left shoulder at the three downed ducks. I was just about to turn around and retrieve them when I heard a distant, but familiar sound. It was as if you held two sticks in your hand and ran down the sidewalk holding the sticks against a picket fence. It was unmistakable, the flat, rapid whop-whop-whop-whop of twin rotors on the big troop helicopters that were being used in the very early years of the Vietnam Conflict.

During the early days of the conflict, many training flights were made over the rural parts of our county. Every teenage boy I knew was very familiar with the distinctive sound. We were fascinated by the brave pilots.

The noise quickly grew louder. I could not see the chopper yet, so I knew it was flying quite low to be so loud and still be hidden by the trees. I could tell it was coming straight toward the opposite end of the ditch and me. As it grew louder and louder, I knew what was going to happen and brought my gun up. Just then the helicopter topped the tree line and was only seconds away from being right over my head. The big side door to the cargo area was open and a crewman was standing there. He was dressed in an olive-green flight suit and a full-body harness. I could clearly see his face. His visor was up on the white flight helmet he wore. The helicopter, because of its sheer size, probably looked lower to the ground than it was, but it was low. Ten seconds more and the chopper would be directly overhead.

As I glanced up to see all this, the noise from the big twin rotors drowned out all other sound. My peripheral vision caught movement at the mouth of the ditch. I instinctively brought the gun to my shoulder as the three ducks boiled out of the thick cover and sprang straight up. As I lined up on the lead bird, my shotgun was aimed right at the open door and the man standing there.

I could see him looking straight down the barrel of my gun and at the scene unfolding below. I waited a half second to let the lead bird fall back some from the speeding machine, and then I pulled the trigger.

I never heard the shot.

The noise of the rotors was deafening, but I saw the first duck fold up. I swung on the last one, which was about even with the rear of the helicopter, and fired again. It, too, fell clean. The backwash from the rotors, in full force now, made it difficult to see as I tried to mark the falling birds when they hit the water. The helicopter seemed to get lower, and the smell of kerosene was strong in the air. My only thought was that I had shot up the fuel tank of a United States Army helicopter that probably had cost a jillion dollars.

Scared to death I watched the chopper fly lower and lower and finally out of sight past the trees. I held my breath. I had seen so many movies, and this was the point in the movie where you see a huge explosion take place with a major fireball erupting into the sky.

The fact that there was no ensuing explosion, no fireball, was only slightly reassuring. The helicopter was riding extremely low, it seemed, and I had shot twice at the chopper, once almost straight into the open cargo door. I had not seen the airman after my first shot. My mind was racing. What was I supposed to do? Make an anonymous call and report a missing helicopter?

As these thoughts went through my mind, I picked up the ducks and headed back to the car. I was absolutely miserable on the ride home. Cleaning the ducks took forever it seemed. I constantly replayed the entire scene in my mind. I could not focus on any of my homework. I didn't sleep a wink all night.

The next day, Wednesday, was a total loss at school. I could not concentrate on anything. All I could think about was seeing that huge helicopter dropping down out of sight after I had emptied my 12-gauge shotgun straight at it. Walking home the half mile from school that afternoon, I drug my feet. I fully expected to find police cars in the driveway, waiting for me.

When none were there, I thought, *Maybe they haven't located the wreckage yet.*

As I went in the backdoor and put my books on the kitchen table, I saw a copy of *The Laurens Advertiser*, our weekly town paper, lying there. The headlines, "Helicopter Makes Emergency Landing at Laurens Airport," took my breath away.

I was doomed. They would find the culprit soon enough.

I read on, "Shortly after takeoff from Greenville Downtown Airport, the Chinook helicopter from Shaw Air Base experienced a leak in a fuel line and had to make an emergency landing at

Laurens County Airport at 4:45 P.M. yesterday afternoon. After repairs were made, the uninjured crew of three took off and returned safely to Greenville Downtown Airport where it was engaged in search and rescue training exercises."

I finally remembered to breathe. I read the story a second time and then a third ".... took off and returned safely" were the sweetest words I have ever read.

I looked at my Timex watch. It was 4:30. I rushed to my room, slipped on my boots, and grabbed my hunting coat, cap, and gun. I had just enough time to see what ducks would pass over the bridge at Little Mountain.

LA ROBE JAUNE*

It was late October, and we were in the middle of an Indian summer. Already there had been some cool weather accompanied by several heavy frosts. We had enjoyed almost a week of warm, but crisp, clear days with bright fall colors. There had also been no rain.

Rabon Creek, perhaps our most favorite duck hunting water, was down. The sandbars, now exposed, were covered with freshly fallen pin oak acorns. It was a splendid Saturday!

Sammy, my fifteen-year-old hunting partner, and I had talked his granddad into dropping us off above the Sandpit so we could duck hunt the Coon Den stretch of Rabon Creek.

Almost every stretch of river we hunted had been given a name long ago. The Coon Den section was midway up Rabon Creek. At the end of the old logging road that lead to this part of the little river was a hollow red oak about as big around as a fifty-five-gallon barrel. Thirty feet up the tree trunk, a missing limb had left a sizeable hole. Many a late evening while one of us quietly leaned up against that old tree and waited on the ducks to float or fly close by, a resident momma coon would lead her late-spring babies out of that hole. If you remained perfectly still, they would pass only a couple of feet away on their nightly trek to the creekside to search for supper.

*The Yellow Dress

111

By the time the truck turned onto the Cold Point Road, Sammy and I had decided that this afternoon it was my turn to be let out first. A half-mile further up Rabon Creek, Sammy would get out and then work his way downriver to the Coon Den where I waited. We would then hunt together toward the Sandpit until Sammy's granddad picked us up right after dark fell.

We always stayed to dusk on our afternoon hunting trips so we could see how many ducks passed the Sandpit going to roost. All the mallards and black ducks roosted on Greenwood Lake and those that flew up Rabon Creek to feed had to pass over the Sandpit near dark to get to the big lake. Before hunting this creek, or any other for that matter, we wanted to know how many ducks were using that stretch of water. We could determine the number by counting the ducks that flew down at dark the previous night.

As long as the acorns remained plentiful, the ducks would return to where they left.

When we stopped on the dirt road at the head of the Coon Den turnoff, I slid out of the faded, dark green 1950 Chevrolet pickup. I took my 12-gauge Browning out of its gun case. As the truck pulled off, I loaded four No. 6 high brass Blue Peter's into the magazine, dropped one more into the barrel, and quietly closed the receiver.

I started down the old logging road. It had been cut in thirty years ago when the original pines had been harvested. The winding dirt road was now once again flanked by nice saw timber, so it was shady and carpeted with long, fresh pine needles.

My quarter-mile walk was so eerily quiet I could not even hear my own footsteps on the soft carpet of pine straw.

Rounding one of the many curves, I was surprised when I came upon a car parked in the middle of the narrow road. It was a late model, sporty, red job with a decal of the letters CHS on the rear window. CHS stood for Clinton High School, our archrival in every respect. The automobile was faintly familiar. It was parked right between two large pines which flanked the road. The road was completely blocked by the car.

It was unusual to see any kind of vehicle on this road. It was strange to see an automobile and not a pickup truck, and it was stranger still that it was obstructing the road.

It was an unwritten rule in the country woods. Do not block a road, no matter how infrequently it is used. During my teenage years, the woods belonged to everyone. Seldom did you see a No Hunting or No Trespassing sign posted. No one with any sense would block a road leading to the river.

I eased past the car, casually glancing through the rolled-up windows, and saw that it was empty. As I passed, I lightly touched the bright red hood. It was slightly warm. The car had not been there for more than an hour, if that.

As I continued walking toward the river, I tried to remember where I had seen that car before. I was wondering why it was in such a strange spot. Anyone familiar with the road would know that there was a large, wide clearing not far down, the remnants of the old logging deck. There was no need to stop in the middle of the narrow dirt road.

Sammy's granddaddy called this logging deck a diddling place. There were always empty beer bottles. There were old tissues, and a few other items we did not ask about, lying around. Sammy and I knew better than to question his granddad what he meant by diddling. We were confident that it had to do with things teenage boys were not supposed to be thinking, but had nonetheless constantly on their minds. In the late 1950s the moral atmosphere in a small southern town was completely different than it is today. I suspect that as much went on in our community as any other place, but in that era many topics were never openly discussed.

As I walked a hundred yards or so further and entered the logging deck clearing, I was even more surprised to see a second car, one I knew well. The older, blue Plymouth sedan belonged to Miss Reshell, my eleventh-grade French teacher.

Decades later when the newer cars were smaller with rounded smooth curves, I worked with a man who still drove an old 1977 Lincoln Mark IV. It was wide and long, and all the young guys at work got to calling that car the Intergalactic Cruiser. Whenever I heard that name it made me remember

Miss Reshell's big blue Plymouth. I could not imagine what Miss Reshell's car was doing at the Coon Den on a Saturday afternoon.

Miss Reshell had moved to our small town two years earlier to take a teaching job at Laurens High School. She lived on Academy Street with an old maid aunt. Miss Reshell was, by at least thirty years, the youngest teacher at our high school. She had gone to college in New Orleans and then lived in France for a while before moving to our town. If the truth be known, she was probably not more than a few years older than I was.

Miss Reshell was very attractive. She had slightly curly dark hair, bright brown eyes, and a figure that every girl at my school would have killed for. If she happened to smile at you, it totally made your day.

Every boy in the school had a crush on her. I suspected the majority held her image tightly in their minds as they drifted off to sleep most nights. I was not immune to her spell. Her first-year French class was very popular among the boys, including myself. I liked her class a lot. That is to say, I liked Miss Reshell a lot, but I did not understand more than a few words of French, which she spoke fluently. I was no better at reading it. Nearing the end of the first six-week period, I had a D average in her class. It was going to be a miracle if I passed her course. Unless I spent a lot more time on French and my grades got a lot better quickly, I would fail.

Inexplicably to me, my mom thought my performance in school was somehow linked to the amount of time I was allowed to roam the woods. The troubling possibility of losing my after-school freedom momentarily clouded an otherwise perfect day as I slipped alongside the driver's side of the Plymouth.

I was now only a step away from the driver's window which was rolled up. Movement in the car caught my eye. This car was not empty. As I took the next step, I saw Miss Reshell raise her back. It was bare! Her head was tilted up slightly as if she was looking at the sky. I was so close I could see small drops of perspiration beaded along her spine. In the harsh, late afternoon sunlight, her damp skin glistened. Her dark hair, where it touched her back, was curling into tight little ringlets. She did not have a stitch of clothes on. Her yellow dress, one she often wore to school, had been tossed on the dashboard. The guy she was sitting astride had only a pair of white socks on. His hands clutched her hips. His eyes were tightly closed.

My eyes, however, were not closed. I thought they were going to bulge out from their sockets.

As Miss Reshell arched her body and leaned back even further, instinctively I stepped away from the car. In doing so, the stock of my gun lightly bumped the driver's door. In the surreal silence of the moment, that little tap on the door could not have sounded any louder or caused a more violent reaction if it had been a stick of dynamite exploding.

As I gaped at the scene taking place in the front seat of the car, Miss Reshell's head jerked around. For one split second her eyes locked onto mine. She pushed herself off and the man fell into the floor of the car, legs up in the air, head under the glove box. His white socks had one red and one blue band around their tops. In one continuous motion, Miss Reshell threw her yellow dress over her head, spun around, slid under the steering wheel, and hit the starter and gas. The engine roared to life.

There they were, Miss Reshell with both hands gripping the steering wheel, buck naked, her dress completely covering her head. The man was scrambling to see what was going on and trying to get up off of the floor. He was cussing up a blue streak. As a young connoisseur of locker room profanity, I was quite impressed.

The motor was now racing. Miss Reshell threw the heavy Plymouth into reverse. The rear tires spun wildly, throwing pine needles and black dirt everywhere as the car tried to gain traction.

I could not move, not a muscle would work. My eyes would not blink, and my breathing seemed to have stopped altogether.

The car shot backward. She turned too far right to make the entrance to the logging road. Instead the car hit a big old-growth sweet gum tree hard, knocking out the left-hand taillight and badly denting the left-hand, rear-quarter panel. Colorful fall leaves and sweet gum balls filled the sky like confetti, showering down on me and the car.

Then the car shot forward. Turning hard right, it centered on a big loblolly pine. Chunks of bark flew everywhere as the front bumper caved in. Pinecones joined the shower of sweet gum balls. Miss Reshell was shifting gears, wrestling the steering wheel, and trying to keep the dress over her head, all at the same time. The car was now somewhat loosely wedged between the sweet gum and pine. The engine got more gas and raced even faster as it shot into reverse again. The sweet gum got a second solid lick. The man, who had made it onto the seat by this time, was thrown back into the floor. Chrome strips fell off the trunk. A hubcap bounced through the trees and out of sight down the hill toward the river.

Again the car shot forward, and I had to jump out of the way, seeking safety behind a big hickory. Bam! The pine got smashed again. Now in reverse once more, the car managed somehow to cross the clearing and onto the road leading out of the logging deck. As the car raced in reverse down the winding road, the yellow dress still covered the driver's head. I knew what was coming, and it didn't take a split second.

There was a resounding crash as that heavy Plymouth plowed into the sports car which was blocking the road to protect their rendezvous. Glass shattered and metal crumpled. I heard doors opening, voices shouting, more cussing, doors slamming, a second motor roaring.

Moments later as the sound of flying gravel faded up Cold Point Road, I stood peering out from behind the hickory tree and remembered to breathe. I could only imagine two completely naked people riding down Cold Point Road trying to decide where and when they were going to stop and put on their clothes. Didn't seem likely they would wait until they pulled into their own driveways.

I was trembling and still looking up the logging road as if the Plymouth might return when I heard two quick gunshots from upriver.

Sammy was into ducks.

Now my mind was racing. What was I supposed to do or say or not say? I waited thirty seconds and shot twice into the air. Grabbing up the empty hulls, I ran as fast as I could in Sammy's direction toward the Coon Den.

Just as I got to the big dead Coon Den tree that overlooked the river, I could see Sammy easing along the bank and around the last curve from upriver. I could barely make out the two greenhead mallards in his left hand. I was trying to control my breathing and think fast.

As Sammy approached he asked, "How many'd you get?"

"None," I said.

"None? Them ducks must've passed not twenty yards out by the time they got here. I was just a short distance upriver when I jumped them. How many did you see?" he asked.

"Three," I guessed.

"Gosh, two must have swung over the hill. Seven got up. I killed two, figured all five would have passed right by you."

"Three did, but I must have been behind them. Never cut a feather," I faked the most disappointment I could muster.

"Well, don't take it so hard," said Sammy. "It'll be okay. Maybe we'll see another group on down. The river's full of acorns, and I'll bet we'll come up on some more."

I put two more shells in my gun, and we turned to go. I let Sammy take the lead. Two curves downriver, we slipped up on another small group of summer ducks. Sammy let me cut out and go around. He was trying to push them by me. I suppose he felt sorry for me, since he already had killed two. After giving me thirty minutes to make my way around the ducks, they flushed. I shot two drakes and let the hen go. Both colorful drakes conveniently drifted into a brush pile on our side of the big creek.

The sky was getting dark when we reached the Sandpit. Two days after full, a large, pale, gibbous moon was working its way up through the afterglow of the autumn day. The creek bottom had turned misty purple. We waited and listened. You could hear the whistle from the wings of the low-flying ducks before you could see them. The highflyers gabbed about where to spend the night. The tan tummies of the males shown in the reflective sunlight from over the horizon.

We counted 146 ducks going to big water. We knew from this that there was some good hunting further up Rabon Creek from the area we had just covered. It would take some footwork to find them.

We continued to walk quietly in the coarse sand of the Sandpit the short distance to the road where Sammy's granddad was waiting. We drove a short while after we turned off Cold Point Road onto the paved road leading to home.

Sammy's granddaddy broke the silence by asking, "Did y'all hear that awful crashing noise not too long after I put you out?"

My heart began to beat hard and fast. I was sure the two people I was wedged between on the narrow seat could hear it thumping. Sammy said, "I sure did. It sounded like it was down-river from me some. I never heard anything like it before. I couldn't tell what it was. At first I thought it was a wreck, but it just kept on crashing and crashing."

Sammy's granddad said, "Where I was waiting down at McPhearson's Bridge, I could hear it good. Johnny, what do you think it was?"

"I didn't hear anything!" I quickly lied.

I hadn't yet decided if I should or could say anything about what I had witnessed to anyone, even Sammy.

Sammy said, "I don't see how you could help but have heard it. It sounded like it was not too far above the Coon Den. It sounded like a demolition derby with cars gettin' all smashed up."

"You probably heard Mr. Ott feeding his cows just across the river. You know how noisy he always is with that tractor at feeding time. I don't think I heard anything but him," I lamely offered.

"What I heard wasn't nobody feeding cows," Sammy said. "It was an awful racket."

My fervent prayer was answered as Sammy abruptly changed the subject saying "Granddad, we saw thirteen groups of big ducks go down, 146 in all, mostly mallards, but a few blacks."

"You boys'll need to go higher up next time. Those ducks may be going as far as Mr. Whitaker's bottoms," his granddad said.

All the way home I was really fretting. I felt somehow I had done something really terrible. I instinctively knew what I had witnessed in that car, but I had never expected I would ever see anything like it. I didn't know what to do, say, or how to act. I certainly couldn't tell my parents.

My worrying continued unabated all through Sunday. In big church that morning I was really singing that part in our Baptist hymn book about "What can wash away my sins? Nothing but the blood of Jesus."

The panic really kicked into gear Monday morning as third-period French class approached. I felt light-headed and my stomach churned. I thought of going straight to the principal's office and telling him I was sick.

I asked Jill, a good friend of mine, after first period, "How was French?"

She said, "Fine."

I asked if she had a substitute for Miss Reshell's class.

Jill said, "No." She looked at me kind of funny, and said that Miss Reshell was there.

Going down the hall at the end of second period I passed Jim, one of my lunchroom buddies, who had French the period right before me.

Still hoping for a miracle, I asked, "Is Miss Reshell here today?"

"Yep, she's here alright. Looking good as ever, too," as he gave me a little wink.

I thought, *If you only knew!*

I stopped at my locker, the water fountain, and the boys' restroom. I lingered at the urinal, trying to decide whether to play the "I'm really sick" line. Finally I decided to bite the bullet and go on to class. I was running late. I prayed the class would have already started, and I could slip in and quietly take my seat without anyone noticing.

The late bell rang, and as luck would have it, Miss Reshell rounded the corner. We reached the door at the same instant.

A little out of breath, she hesitated a moment and said, "Good morning, Johnny," and went in.

"Morning, Miss Reshell" I said softly to her back as I followed her in the door. I could not keep my mind from seeing in vivid detail her damp, bare body. I could feel my face flush. My head began to throb. I buried my face in my book the whole fifty minutes. When I took a peek, Miss Reshell seemed even more nervous than I felt. She did not glance my way or even call on anyone in my row. Deliverance came as the bell rang for lunch.

In the cafeteria, Sammy and I sat with Dave, Jim, and Larry, all big jocks on the football team.

Dave, with a mouth full of mashed potatoes, asked, "Did you see Miss Reshell's car this morning? Must have had one bad wreck. The front and back of her car are tore up bad."

Jim chimed in, "That Plymouth of hers is messed up for sure. Lights out, rear smashed in, hubcap missing. They talk about us teenagers being bad drivers."

I was staring a hole in my pale green, plastic, partitioned plate and said nothing. I made up my mind right then I was never going to tell a soul, not even Sammy. Not ever.

As the week wore on, each day in French class got a little easier. Miss Reshell seemed not quite so nervous. She put her car in Sherer's Body Shop to be fixed.

In third period she never looked my way during class, and no one within three seats of me ever got called on. Friday's weekly French test seemed particularly hard to me, but of course I had given up all hope of passing French now. I was sure it would be hopeless.

On the following Monday, Miss Reshell's repaired car was in its usual parking place. She came into class wearing her yellow dress.

The yellow dress!

I almost passed out. I started hyperventilating. Visions of Miss Reshell without anything on, not just in my imagination, but for real, continually invaded my mind like an endless film loop being played over and over and over. I was sure everyone else in class could read my mind. God was going to strike me stone, graveyard dead right there on the spot.

The class began as usual. Miss Reshell handed out the test papers from the previous Friday. She said she was very disappointed in the scores and that we all needed to study harder. She called out the names of each person, as was the custom. One by one the students walked to the front and got their test paper. You could tell how each person had done as they returned to their seats. The look on their faces told the story.

I knew my score was going to be low when Jackie Thompson made a face as she got her paper. Jackie was the smartest person at Laurens High. She always made good grades. Not surprisingly, my

name was called last. As I walked to the front I glued my eyes on the floor. Miss Reshell had moved to the rear of her big oak desk, and I had to pass her desk to get to where she stood. As I reached for my paper and started to take it, it fell from her hand. We both stooped to pick it up at the same instant. For just a moment we were hidden from the class. Miss Reshell picked up the paper first. As I tried to take it, she held it a fraction of a second causing me to look into her eyes.

She lifted her finger to her lips, silently motioning "Shhhhh."

With the faintest of smiles, she released the test paper and I returned to my seat holding the first A+ I had ever gotten in French!

The pact with the devil was sealed. There was now a conspiracy of silence.

I kept everything to myself, and the A+s on my French tests continued. Mom and Dad were quite impressed with my next report card, particularly with my improvement in French.

The next time that Sammy and I hunted the Coon Den it was early December. The temperature hovered at thirty-four degrees with low-hanging clouds and a stiff northerly breeze. Sammy said it was my turn to go upriver and his turn to go to the tree, but I said no. I said I needed to redeem myself from my last Coon Den trip. He laughed and gave in.

On my way to the Den this time there were no cars. I picked up the broken pieces of light lenses, chrome strips, and even located the hubcap. I found a big stump hole. I put the evidence in there and covered it all with a foot of pine straw.

A fifteen-minute wait after I reached the big, old Coon Den tree, I heard Sammy shoot. Within seconds four acorn-filled mallards flew down river. As they climbed for altitude and passed by me at eye level I got my first triple of the season. When Sammy got to the Coon Den tree, I was wading on tiptoes back across Rabon Creek. My third duck, an old gray hen, had fallen across the creek. I had to wade the cold, fast water to retrieve her.

As I scrabbled up the slick bank, naked from the waist down, Sammy smiled, "Water cold?"

It was a tired joke, but I gave the stock answer to the stock question, "Cold as a witch's titty."

"Thank goodness the river's down," I said. "When it gets to you-know-where, it takes me a while to get over it."

I glanced up at Sammy and smiled a little. Sammy knowingly agreed "Boy, you can say that again!"

We both chuckled. I dried off with my jockey underwear and put on my pants. I shoved my wet underwear in my hunting jacket along with the ducks. I pulled on my hunting pants and very carefully pulled up the brass zipper. Zipping up without any underwear on was a delicate operation. You only forget once.

Sammy had two nice mallards in his hand and as he watched me lace up my boots, I bragged a little on my triple.

"Your shooting's improving almost as much as your French scores, old buddy," Sammy teased. "You must be burning the midnight oil on that French" he said.

My unearned grades, along with Mom and Dad's praise, actually inspired me to study more. As I worked harder, everything began to make sense, and I started to really like French. The more I liked it, the more I studied.

"I'm kinda getting the hang of it," I said to Sammy. "I like it a lot better and it's coming a lot easier for me."

"I can't wait till next year to take Miss Reshell's class. That lady sure is easy on the eyes," Sammy said.

As usual we hunted on down to the Sandpit where we met Sammy's granddad.

Duck hunting season closed on New Year's. The days grew colder, and studying came up against less competition. I began really earning the As and A+s in French. I determined to make it my best subject for the rest of the year.

For some unknown reason, the powers that be in our high school decided in late spring of 1961 to award letters, not just for sports, but also for outstanding performance in academics. On Awards Day near the last day of school, I found myself standing on the stage in our auditorium with some of the really bright students in my grade.

I heard the principal announce "Carolyn Cliatt – English." Applause.

"Gene Ott – math." More applause.

"Johnny Faris – French."

Just as the others had done, I crossed the stage to the principal. He handed me a crisp certificate and bright gold block letter L.

I had lettered in French!

As I moved toward the end of the stage, I cut my eyes to the front row which was the faculty section, and there was Miss Reshell. I think she was proud that I had earned my letter and greatly relieved that I had kept her secret. She gave me a big smile which totally made my day!

In late May, I was double-dating at the Laurens drive-in movie. I saw the red sports car with the letters CHS on the rear window, again. It, too, had been fixed. As casually as I could, I asked my date if she recognized the red car, parked one row in front of us. She looked over her shoulder and said it belonged to a senior on the football team in Clinton. She added that he had been going steady with one of our cheerleaders for well over a year.

Steady, right! I thought.

I never got a look at anyone in the red sports car that night of the movie. Its windows were so steamed up it looked like a cold morning fog had settled in the front seat. But I would have bet a Coca-Cola no one in that car was wearing *la robe jaune*.

THE BEST DAY EVER

I stood in the chilly salt water on the South Carolina beach. I had to keep shifting my weight as the receding waves tugged the coarse, sea-washed sand from under my bare feet. My faded khaki pants were rolled up to my knees.

It was in the late afternoon, and the purple-and-black storm clouds were still at my back. I was looking due east at the clear horizon. In the back of my mind I added my sighting of the thirty-third southbound Navy ship to the day's list.

At that moment, the first good strike of the trip almost knocked the surf rod out of my hand.

It was October 28. It was a day I would remember the rest of my life.

Our nation, and the world, would not easily forget the events of this day either. The year was 1962.

We had enjoyed cool, clear weather for over a week with just enough wood smoke, fading leaf colors, and early morning frost to let us know fall was losing its grip and giving over to early winter.

The preceding months of summer were always my dad's most hectic time at the glass bottle plant where he worked. From my youngest years I was taught that people drink a lot more soft drinks in the warm weather. Coca-Cola, Pepsi, Orange Crush, and other soda bottles that were made in the glass factory were in highest demand in the hot, sticky days of our southern summers. The plant ran full-steam during this, their busiest season.

Now summer had passed, and I had been subtly suggesting a fishing trip since early September. By October Dad was ready for a break, so on Monday morning he announced that we were going surf fishing that coming Saturday.

The plan was to get up Saturday morning at 3:30 A.M. and drive the five hours to Pawleys Island, South Carolina, our traditional fishing and vacation spot. We would meet our longtime fishing friend Esther Johnson, load our fishing gear into her rusted-out, four-by-four International Scout, and drive up to the nearly deserted and undeveloped Litchfield Beach. We would have several miles of pristine surf all to ourselves.

In the autumn the northeasters blew hard, transforming the swimmer-safe surf of summer into rough, strong currents and deeply cut, steep sloughs. Prime channel bass haunts were born of these fall storms.

The stable weather we had been enjoying all week almost guaranteed fresh fillets for the next fish fry. That was the plan.

Dad and I spent a lot of time each night during the week leading up to our adventure getting out the right clothes, some for a warm day, some for the potentially cool morning. We cleaned and oiled our reels and loaded fresh fifteen-pound test line onto the spools of the four Penn casting reels. We packed the barely used surf rods that Dad had made all by himself less than a year ago. Finally, we got out a cooler for soft drinks and snacks and made sure we had an extra cooler so we could pack fish on ice for the trip home.

I was secretly hoping to catch a nice spot tail bass.

Fishermen are eternally optimistic.

After much preparation, everything was packed by Thursday night. I was extremely excited. I loved spending time with my dad. He was always my best friend, and we were going to get to spend all day Saturday together, the first time we had been able to do so in several months.

The rain began early Friday morning. It did not stop all day. School was a total loss. I was so worked up about Saturday and so worried about the weather that I could not concentrate on a thing. Thank goodness I had no tests.

When I finally got home from school my mom said she was sorry about our trip. She said she knew Dad and I were really counting on it. To be encouraging, Mom said she knew Dad would work hard to find a time he could reschedule. She tried to lift my spirits, but I was sick with disappointment.

Dad got home from work a little earlier than usual. He came in, shook the rain off his hat, and said to my mom, "Harriett can we have supper a little early? Johnny and I have to get up very early in the morning."

Those were the sweetest words I had ever heard in all of my seventeen years.

Dad turned to me and said, "Let's throw in some wet weather gear. It might be raining tomorrow."

My mom looked at my dad like he had lost his mind. I looked at him as if he was the key figure in the Second Coming. Before anyone could change their mind, I quickly descended into the basement to find the foul weather gear.

I heard my mom say to my dad, "If you two come down with pneumonia you are going to have to nurse each other. I'm not looking after two people who have completely taken leave of their senses. Besides," she asked, "have you been listening to the news?"

I heard Dad say "Harriett, I know the weather is terrible, and the news sounds really bad, but there's not much we can do about either one. I'm going to take the boy fishing."

The storm clouds that threatened our fishing trip were caused by a cold front that had begun two weeks earlier in western Canada. About the same time, but far to the south, a different kind of storm was brewing, one that had developed into a national state of emergency.

This political crisis had originated on October 14, off the tip of Florida. High-flying reconnaissance planes out of Opa-Locka, Florida, had delivered photos of Soviet missiles under construction in Cuba. One week later on October 22, President John F. Kennedy announced the discovery on national radio and television. He immediately ordered a blockade around the island of Cuba in order to keep the Soviet Union from off-loading any more missiles.

The Soviets attempting such a provocative action was motivated by the fact that in late 1961 the Soviet Union found itself desperately behind the United States in the arms race. Soviet missiles were not powerful enough to reach the United States; however the missiles that the United States had in place could potentially strike every corner of the Soviet Union.

According to the news, Soviet Premier Nikita Khrushchev conceived the idea of placing his intermediate range missiles in Cuba. Three days after President Kennedy had imposed the initial naval blockade around Cuba, he significantly expanded the blockade. Throughout this Cuban missile crisis, U.S. military readiness was raised to DEFCON 2, a condition of national defense readiness that was only one step away from nuclear war.* Never before had our nation been put on such a high alert.

*Wikipedia: The Free Encyclopedia, "Cuban Missile Crisis," October 3, 2012.

The newspaper account continued that with the island nation surrounded, the Russians sent a letter on September 26, 1962, proposing that the Soviet missiles and personnel would be removed if the U.S. would guarantee not to invade Cuba. Everyone on both sides of the Atlantic held their breath.

Mom and Dad continued to discuss the latest news while I found all the wet weather gear we owned and stuffed it in a separate canvas duffel bag my dad used when he served in the Navy during World War II. I lugged it upstairs to be packed.

Mom finished cooking supper in silence. She didn't have much to say at the table. Dad was trying his best to follow the school gossip being relayed by my two sisters, Gregory, fourteen, and Harriett, eleven years old.

I wolfed down one of my most favorite meals, chipped beef on white bread toast and butter-laced Cream of Wheat. I never failed to clean my plate, no matter what Mom fixed. She was a terrific cook. I also kept a sharp eye out for anything my sisters, who ate like birds, might not consume. If there was something left, I would ask for that, too. I could never seem to get enough. Mom said I was the only one she had ever seen who could eat a huge supper and one hour later eat two peanut butter and jelly sandwiches.

After supper, Dad and I set two alarm clocks. This precaution turned out to be totally unnecessary because I never went to sleep. I rolled over every thirty minutes to see if it was time to get up. Finally, at 3:30 A.M., after rushing all the gear into the car through a torrential downpour, Dad with a cup of hot coffee in his hand, started the car, turned the windshield wipers on, and we rolled out of the driveway. It was raining so hard Dad had to turn the headlights on low beam. When he tried to see if high beams would help the visibility, it was like staring at a solid wall of water.

I prayed a silent prayer, *God please let the rain stop. Please let us catch some fish, and please keep Mom and the girls, and us, safe.*

It would not be the last time that day I prayed.

The rain made the driving difficult. The two-lane road seemed narrower than usual. The oncoming traffic that time of morning was light, but the wet pavement and rain made the oncoming headlights blinding. We took it slow and easy on Highway 76 into Columbia, down Bull Street, past the State Mental Hospital, and over the Wateree Swamp. We turned off onto Highway 261. The eastern sky grudgingly gave up the night as we rolled into Manning and our regular breakfast stop at the Center Café.

Dad paid ten cents for a newspaper to go with some scrambled eggs, crispy bacon, four pieces of generously buttered toast, grits, and more hot coffee. I had the same except I substituted good, cold milk for the coffee.

The shocking bold headline of the morning paper read:
U-2 PLANE SHOT DOWN OVER CUBA
This incident of a United States spy plane flying over sovereign air space and the pilot, Major Rudolf Anderson, being killed, pushed both sides even closer to war.

Dad read every line of the article as he finished his third cup of coffee. He read aloud, "Khrushchev has sent a second letter demanding the removal of U.S. missiles in Turkey in exchange for the removal of Soviet missiles in Cuba."

He said to me, "This thing might get pretty rough."

I could tell that Dad was more worried than he was letting on. At seventeen I was only a few months shy of the draft age. If war was declared, a boy my age would be at the top of the list. A volunteer army was adequate during peacetime, but when war broke out and the nation needed a lot more soldiers, there would be a national call-up of eligible young men. The admissible age was eighteen.

Dad had seen war up close. During World War II he had survived a convoy crossing of the North Atlantic. His ship was shot out from under him in the Mediterranean, he spent a year in the newly built Bethesda hospital in Maryland with a broken neck, and he later received the Purple Heart.

At Dad's request a close friend who worked in the personnel department in the Pentagon doctored Dad's medical records so he could go back to sea, though his injuries were so severe that his medical records had recommended he not be allowed back on active duty.

As gunnery officer, he fought all the way across the Pacific on the aircraft carrier USS *Bennington*. His ship, like many others, ended up in Tokyo Bay when the Japanese signed the documents of surrender. Much of Japan was in ruins and many of the civilian population had been killed by the numerous raids from bombs dropped by the planes off of the aircraft carriers. Following the surrender, it was important to take physical control of the nation, particularly the cities such as Tokyo. Manpower for security duty was scarce. My dad was placed in charge of a group of ordinary sailors from the ship who were acting as shore patrol in the devastated city of Tokyo.

I had been shown a number of times, an old black-and-white photograph of Dad and his brother Teedy, who was also in the Navy. They were being served a drink by a Japanese butler in a starched white jacket on the veranda of the Imperial hotel. In the picture, this stately building was the only edifice standing as far as the eye could see. Dad said many times that he did not know why the shore patrol was even needed because there was nothing and no one within fifty miles. Tokyo had been bombed for weeks. The city had been burned to the ground.

Dad and Mom, along with other parents their age, knew the dangers of war firsthand. They worried about their own sons who would be called upon to fight if a new war began.

But I, along with my friends, mostly lived in unspoken, but ever-present fear, with the imagined horror of a hydrogen hell.

At the movie theater we had watched and re-watched news-reels of nuclear tests in the Nevada desert. We had seen footage of Russian bomber squadrons, flying practice missions high above Siberia, their contrails streaming. Old, scratchy black-and-white clips of mushroom clouds rising over Hiroshima and Nagasaki played a prominent role in these films.

We had neighbors on the corner of Farley Avenue and Pine Street who installed a prefab bomb shelter in their side yard and stocked it with canned goods and water. That didn't help our peace of mind.

Oh yeah, I worried, just like my parents. I would be way out in the country hunting or fishing and I'd look up and see one of those white, expanding vapor trails from a plane flying so high that I could not even make it out.

I wondered if it was a Soviet bomber, slipping through our radar defenses and headed to the Savannah River Plant. The bomb plant, as it was called, was where all of the weapons-grade plutonium in the United States was produced. It was the perfect target, and it was not far upwind from my hometown.

And in spite of that soggy morning and the bad news, dad and I both stowed our unshared, secret fears and got back in the car. The rain fell even harder, but the sleepy, gray light of first dawn made the driving easier.

As we traveled, we talked about all the things I wanted to talk about. Dad steered the conversation to the subjects he knew were of interest to me.

As we moved on down Highway 521 through Greeleyville, Salters, and Andrews, Dad and I discussed college, what I might like to do, and what I thought my life's work would be.

We talked about future duck hunting trips, plans to build an offshore fishing boat, the purchase of a new Labrador retriever pup to train, and of course, the adventure of the day ahead.

As we rolled into Georgetown, South Carolina, two surprises awaited us. The cold weather front that had been moving across the state from west to east was stalled directly over Georgetown. We passed through the last of the rain at Nine Mile Curve and broke into a crystal clear Tiffany-blue sky on Market Street. It was as if an imperceptible hand was holding back the wall of rain clouds, right over the sleepy harbor town only thirteen miles east of our destination. The fast-changing, unpredictable coastal weather was breaking in our favor for the moment.

Dad and I looked at each other as we sat at the first red light and grinned like two mules eating briars.

I whispered a prayer, *Thank you, Lord.*

As we approached the drawbridge where the Waccamaw River and Intracoastal Waterway become one, the bridge was already open. There was a pretty good line waiting. Strangely, all the drivers and passengers of the waiting cars and trucks were out of their vehicles and lined up on the water's edge, watching whatever it was that had brought the traffic to a standstill. I did not take this to be a good sign. I had seen the drawbridge open and close many times with cars backed up and waiting, but never before had I seen anyone get out to watch what was causing such a delay.

Dad put the car in park, cut off the engine, and we joined the crowd. If I live to be a hundred, I will never forget the spectacle I witnessed for the next hour. It was our nation preparing for a full-scale invasion. To my great surprise, there was, as far as the eye could see, east all the way down Winyah Bay, and west up the Intracoastal Waterway, a vast number of Navy landing craft. The seemingly endless line appeared as a gray ribbon stretching through the yellow-green saw grass marsh of the river delta. The boats were no more than a hundred yards apart and traveling as fast as their stubby shapes and powerful diesel engines could propel them.

An old man leaning over the bridge railing answered my Dad's first question. "The bridge opened this morning at 7:15," he said.

People stood in small groups and talked as the spectacle snaked south. Bos'n mates navigating the landing craft waved up at the growing crowd, and we waved back.

Shouts of "God Bless!"

"Give'm hell!"

And "Good luck!" were mostly swallowed up in the rumble of the heavy diesel marine motors.

World War II veterans in their mid-forties were telling younger men about their experiences of huddling on one of those craft and waiting to step off into a promised watery grave far away on the beaches in France or on some unnamed island in the Pacific.

My dad just watched and listened in silence. He never spoke of the war, but I had seen the pain of war in him. His neck and head injuries had caused blinding headaches for many years after the war.

When I was very young, on more than one occasion I saw Dad sensing a spell coming on. He fell to his knees, pulling the heavy black telephone off the table while trying to call my Mom. The phone would crash to the floor as he passed out. Being the oldest child, I tried to help my dad as my little sisters cried.

At 10:30 A.M. the last landing craft passed, the bridge swung closed, and Dad and I got back in the car.

I said, "Dad, I didn't know that there were that many landing craft in the world. We're going to invade Cuba, aren't we?"

He looked at me, smiled, and said, "Let's go catch some fish."

We arrived at Esther's trailer thirty minutes later.

Esther managed the Pawleys Island Pier for a man in New York who owned the then for-pay public pier. He furnished Esther a place to live right next to the pier. Her trailer sat on a high oceanfront sand dune, commanding perhaps the finest view of the Atlantic to be found on the island.

As we drove up, we found Esther was fiddling with something under the hood of her ten-year-old faded yellow International Scout. As we climbed out of our car she slammed down the hood of the beach buggy.

"Watching that big front rolling in, I thought you two might have decided not to come," she said as we shook hands. Her hands were small but strong, rough and weathered, as are the hands of most people who work outdoors a lot.

Barely five feet tall, Esther was wide at the shoulders and built like a fireplug. She had never married, and she lived with her aging mother and stepfather. I never knew another woman that was as good as Esther at hunting or fishing. Actually, I did not know many men who were her equal with a shotgun or surf rod. As the years wound past, she taught me many things about hunting and fishing. She became a lifelong friend.

"I'm all loaded. Y'all put your stuff in the back. There's room for your surf rods in the rack on the front bumper. I'll just grab the bait out of the fridge, and we'll be ready. The tide's about an hour and a half up, but we have plenty of good water left," she said as she disappeared into the trailer. The screen door slammed shut behind her.

I climbed the soft sand the few remaining yards to the highest point on the dune and looked out over the autumn beach, scrubbed clean by the high tide. The clear jade-green breakers were backlit by the sun as they curled and gave up their tops to the northeast wind.

The gulls were frantically feeding over the finger mullet which were schooled up and headed south just outside the breakers.

There was great promise in the warm sunshine mixed with the crisp, cool breeze.

Esther called me to come on. She was loaded and ready. As I turned to get in the Scout, I noticed a large gray ship on the horizon. It, like the schooling mullet, was pushing hard south.

The three of us climbed into Esther's vehicle amid tackle boxes, coolers, rain gear, boots, a minnow trap, a cast net, and at least an inch of sand in the floorboard.

The sand was not nearly as deep in the front on the passenger's side where Dad was sitting. For several years a sizeable and growing hole had rusted through the floor. You could push the sand with your foot and kind of herd it through the hole. However, it was important to remember to place your foot over the hole when you hit the beach or the soft, damp sand spinning off the front right tire would just force more sand right back in.

Five miles north, Esther turned off U.S. Route 17 at a big new sign for Litchfield Beach that read:

> Beautiful Litchfield Beach
> Oceanfront Lots
> From $4,900.00

My dad said to Esther, "I wish I could have bought one of those lots a few years ago."

I remembered the day well when my mom, dad, and I were sitting in the backseat of a big, black Cadillac driven by Mr. Boyles. His daughter, Jean Boyles Brading, was sitting in the front seat. Jean was my mom's roommate at Converse College in 1936. At that time Mr. Boyles owned a large part of Litchfield Beach. As we rode down the recently paved, narrow tar-and-gravel road that paralleled the beach, there were fresh wooden stakes with numbers stenciled on them placed every one hundred feet.

As I sat between Mom and Dad in the backseat and watched large, high, untouched sand dunes roll by on the left, Mr. Boyles said, "Harriett, Jean and I want you and Johnny to pick out a lot. We are keeping #43 through #53 for our family, but you can have first choice of any of the rest for $2,500."

I remember later hearing my dad tell my mom that even if they could afford it, he did not think it was such a good investment. He added he had been fishing that beach since the mid-1930s, and nothing had ever been built there and probably never would.

As Esther turned right onto the beach road today, I could see there were only a handful of cottages clustered near the entrance road. The beach heading south and north was the same as in my very early childhood when I came here with Dad fishing. The survey stakes along the road were now weathered gray, and the lot numbers were faded.

The beach that day was a far cry from the wall-to-wall condos and summer houses that cover every square inch of buildable land on this stretch of coast now in 2012.

Even with the four-wheel drive Scout, we could not find a place to cross the impressive dunes. So, as was our custom, Esther drove south almost the same distance we had driven north on U.S. Route 17. When we approached the inlet separating Litchfield and Pawleys Island, we turned onto the beach at the water's edge and headed back north again, this time driving right along the surf. Now the four-wheel beach buggy was earning its keep.

Esther drove just below the high-water mark. We moved slowly while looking at the surf. It was a little past halfway to flood stage. The way the waves broke over the outer bars would tell us where to stop.

We paralleled the ocean for at least two miles north before Esther and Dad both agreed on a great-looking spot. Even my less experienced eye could tell this stretch of water looked best. The beach dropped off so severely that Esther, some distance back, had to power the Scout up all the way above the sand shelf. The slough ran at least a couple hundred yards long. It was so deep there was a two-foot vertical drop-off at the high-water mark. The beach sloped from there very steeply into the crashing waves. The submerged sandbar forming the outer edge of this natural bait trap was sixty yards offshore at this stage of the tide.

Esther swung the nose of the vehicle toward the dunes, put it in reverse, and backed us right up to the edge of where the tide would come. Dad and I took off our shoes and socks and rolled up our pants legs. Esther was barefooted and wearing shorts. I do not remember more than a handful of times ever seeing her dressed any other way.

Esther dropped the tailgate and opened up the tackle boxes. Dad and I began removing the surf rods from the front-bumper rod rack, bringing them to the rear, and using the tailgate as a waist-high work bench. We started attaching the wire leader and sliding sinker rigs to the swivels already attached to the fifteen-pound test line.

Esther's two long rods stayed rigged so while we were getting our four rods ready she began to fillet the foot-long, six-hour-old mullet she had caught early that morning on the dead low tide.

As she handed us the baits, we threaded the mullet strips on the hooks and attached three-ounce pyramid sinkers to the three-foot wire leader.

We were ready.

I picked up one of the rod holders Dad had made, and I walked down the beach thirty yards. By using the rod holder, or sand spike as they are called, we could fish more than one rod at a time and still keep the rods and reels safely above the salty waves. Esther was staking out the area directly behind the Scout for her two rods, and Dad was walking up the beach to make his first cast.

With the heavy sinker and bait swinging on the end of the long leader, I took the reel out of gear, pressing my thumb tightly against the line, and waded out a few feet into the waves. No matter how warm the air was, that first wave breaking on my bare legs felt icy. It didn't take long, though, before I got used to the water and then, oddly, the water actually felt warmer than the crisp breeze.

I decided to take it easy on my first cast. It had been a few months since I last used these rods. No use making a bad throw and having a backlash the very first thing.

The slough looked so deep I did not believe it was going to be of much advantage anyway.

I set my first rig out without making a fool of myself and adjusted the sand spike into the damp sand a few feet above where the last wave had run out of steam climbing the steep beach. I reeled in a few feet of line to take up the slack, tested the drag, and set the rod into the rod holder.

After watching the rod tip for a couple of minutes to see how the sinker was holding, I started back to the Scout for my second rod. Esther was already casting number two, and Dad was headed back for his other rod.

When all three of us had the six rods set, we met at the Scout. We unloaded the coolers and set up three folding chairs.

Dad and Esther sat down with a cup of coffee that poured steaming out of a large, silver thermos that Esther produced from under the piles of equipment on her backseat. I knew from past fishing trips that this would be the time when they would visit and catch up on old times until one or both of them got their first strike.

I was way too excited to settle down and fish like that, not today at least.

I had waited so long for this day to come, then hoped so hard that the rain would stop. Now that we were here, I was going to fish and fish hard.

I only put both my rods in the sand spikes long enough to change baits. Otherwise, I was holding one rod and constantly watching the bending tip of my second.

Traditional wisdom held that you would hook more channel bass, spot tails we called them, if you did not hold the rod.

The big bass were famous for picking up the mullet fillets and carrying them a few feet before fully getting the bait and hook in their mouths. With the rod in the sand spike, the three-foot leader would slide through the heavy lead sinker without any unnatural pull or weight for the fish to notice.

Conversely, quite often, if you were holding the rod when you felt the fish pick up the bait, it would dramatically telegraph up the line to your hand. Then you would almost always instinctively try to set the hook. This sent an undesirable signal back down the line to the fish that all was not right, and he would promptly spit out the bait.

However, in my case, the excitement of sensing the fish take the bait was more than enough to make me take the risk. Besides, I could feel an old blue crab peck, peck, pecking away at my bait. I could sense the sinker rolling if it was not holding in the strong current, and I could tell if seaweed or trash was on the line. All these things would make the bait less attractive to a big fish. If I was holding my rod, I could solve the problem more quickly.

Eleven-thirty came and went. Then twelve-thirty, and none of us had even a decent nibble.

Esther switched to a smaller double-hook rig on her lighter rod and with some fresh shrimp caught six nice half-pound blues in rapid succession.

By now everyone was hungry. Esther scrambled around in the back of the Scout, located the white gas Coleman stove, and turned the tailgate into a kitchen. The big, heavy, black cast-iron frying pan was stored in an oil-soaked brown paper grocery bag. Cooking oil, salt, pepper, two fresh lemons, and half-a-sack of new red potatoes were transported in a shallow wooden box.

With her razor-sharp fillet knife, Esther made quick work of cleaning the half-dozen blues. She salted both sides and added a generous coating of black pepper. She cut the lemons thin and placed two slices on top of each fillet. An aluminum foil pouch was formed for each fish. They were tightly wrapped, and were placed around the edge of the stove's grate.

Esther washed the potatoes in the salty ocean water, cut them into quarters, and dropped them into the frying pan full of hot oil. Just minutes later the sizzling bluefish fillets were flipped out of their tin foil boats onto dark blue speckled enamel plates. Generous portions of steaming hot, crispy potatoes landed alongside with a little more black pepper and a sprinkle of vinegar. It was every man for himself.

There are few things better than fish that fresh, cooked within yards of where they were caught. I ate like a savage. There was no use looking to see if any leftovers remained. Only the oily smudges glistening in the sunlight gave indication that the plates had even been used.

While Esther put a fresh pot of coffee on the little stove, I took the plates and frying pan to the water's edge. I scrubbed each one with the clean, wet sand and rinsed them in the cool salt water. I set the plates on the hood of the Scout to dry in the breeze, but Esther dried the heavy iron skillet, wiped on a coat of cooking oil and carefully wrapped it back up in the brown paper bag.

Even though none of us had a big strike yet, we all had eaten with one eye still trained on our rod tips. If a big bass hit, it would be a footrace to the rod before the fish pulled it and the sand spike into the water.

Lunch over, we all changed to fresh bait, recast our lines, and settled in with a cup of fresh, steaming coffee, mine with lots of sugar and evaporated milk.

It was clear that a ton of blues were in the slough. I was tempted to switch one rod over to a smaller double-hook rig and go after them with fresh shrimp. That would, however, cut my chances of catching a big bass by fifty percent, a concession I was not willing to make even for catching scrappy bluefish two at a time.

For several years I had dreamed of catching an award-winning spot tail bass. These fish had many names including: puppy drum, red drum, bull bass, red fish, and channel bass. On our part of the coast we called them spot tail bass. Every year the

Chamber of Commerce for the Grand Strand gave out citations for a number of different species of saltwater fish found in the Carolina waters. The fish of each species had to meet a certain weight minimum to qualify for the prized certificates they issued. To make it a challenge, the minimum was set pretty high. The cutoff weight for spot tail bass was twenty pounds, a very nice bass for our neck of the woods. I had never caught one that large.

Dad and Mom went to Pawleys Island on their honeymoon in 1944 and had never since taken a family beach vacation at any other place. Dad had fished these beautiful waters for a long time, and even he had only caught a couple of bass that big.

Fishing was slow this day. The pending low-pressure system was really effecting the fish.

I prayed another little prayer, *Lord, just one nice fish. Maybe not a citation fish, but a good fish. Just one.*

As the minutes slipped by, I kept looking over my shoulder to see what the storm that was held captive was doing. I continued counting the ships steaming southward.

When Dad and I ended up at the Scout to get bait or a snack at the same time, I would point to the latest silhouette on the horizon and ask, "What kind of ship is that one, Dad?"

He would squint his eyes, pause a minute as if replaying some mind movie, and say, "It's a heavy cruiser."

At another time, he might say, "It's an oiler."

Or again, "It's a destroyer."

Dad could identify them all. I knew that as he looked out over the vast, whitecapping sea, those ships stirred both pride in his past and concern for his son's future.

The afternoon was about done. The tide had crested and was now falling back into the slough. The water looked even better than when we arrived. The falling water had cleaned up the surf some. The water was clearer and was looking better every minute. But it was late. We were running out of time, and the storm clouds looked as if they were beginning to overpower the high pressure that had been holding them back all day.

Esther and Dad were still fishing, but they were beginning to put a few things back into the Scout, a sure sign that time was limited.

I returned up the beach to the truck to get fresh bait.

Dad said, "Let's fish these baits out, and then I expect we'd better head in."

Esther cut up a fresh mullet and gave me the two best pieces, one for each rod. I started back to where my rods were. A few steps from the Scout I heard Esther say to Dad, "I wish he would catch just one nice fish. I've never seen anyone fish harder."

I put the fresh mullet in the little cups Dad had welded on each sand spike to hold extra weights, hooks, and bait. I reeled in my first rod and removed the old bait. The meat was gone, courtesy of a blue crab, no doubt. Just the tough skin remained. I discarded this, and it had scarcely touched the ground when a big gull swooped down, picked it up, and started a ruckus with half-a-dozen of its cousins.

I carefully put the fresh mullet on, being sure the hook's sharp point was exposed through the fresh flesh and tough skin.

The slough wasn't nearly as wide or long now with the tide going out. In the clearing water I could make out for the first time a break in the outer sandbar from which the water was rapidly flowing. This funnel is often called a rip, and it is a natural feeding spot. I had been unable to see it an hour earlier.

I took my best shot and laid the new offering within two yards of the funnel mouth. The weight hit the water; then the mullet followed. As usual, I could feel the weight catch hold of the bottom. I began to take in a little slack. Another ship, number thirty-three by my count, was in my peripheral vision when a strike like a bolt of lightning shot up my line and bent the light surf rod dangerously low to the water.

There was no slow pickup and mouthing of the bait by this strike. Whatever hit the bait had done so before the bait had ever reached the bottom, and it had done so with total conviction. I forgot all about letting the fish run and waiting to set the hook. My instincts took over, and I hauled back hard. Line melted off the reel, and I followed it into the ocean just to take pressure off the rig.

I could see Esther racing down the beach as fast as her short, stubby legs would carry her. She got to my second rod and started winding in the line as she shouted, "Let off on the drag a little, that's a big fish! Might be a big shark or ray, but you've got to let him have his head. Whatever he wants to do, let him go."

My heart sank a little. *Shark? Ray? No!*

I wanted my catch to be a big wide-shoulder bass. I turned the drag another half turn to loosen up a little and started to follow the fish down the slough. Line was still easing off the reel, but not as fast since I was walking him down the beach.

The fish, or shark, or whatever it was, was headed to the north end of the long slough. Since I had seen the big funnel, I did not think there would be another opening in the bar in the direction the fish was headed. We were now fifty yards north of where the fish first struck. Careful to keep my line tight, I was basically walking faster than the fish was swimming so I could gain a little of my line. Another twenty yards and the fish must have been able to sense the outflow of water in the opposite direction. He abruptly changed course and headed south. I watched him swim right to the inside edge of the outer bar. I thought he was going to try to cross it, but water over the sand-bar was now getting skinny. He thought better of that route and headed back, powering south.

I had gained a good bit of my lost line on the course rever-sal. Even though the water was clearer and not as deep, I still could not see the phantom that was more than holding up its end of this tug-of-war.

Esther and Dad had successfully reeled in all five lines with-out them becoming tangled with mine. Now they were close at hand with lots of advice.

Just then my line began to rise in the water. A big square tail, two hands wide and glowing burnished bronze in the late afternoon sun, cleared the surface. A single distinct black spot the size of a quarter was centered on the tail.

No shark, no throw-back stingray, but the largest spot tail bass I had ever hooked was slugging it out with me. My excite-ment level jumped several notches, knowing I had hooked a real trophy bass. It was flavored with the fear I might possibly lose him.

I could feel the fish begin to pick up speed as he drew nearer to the outflow. Every minute the fish was on, the tide was falling and the rip was picking up steam. The current would be sub-stantial in the outflow. The fish knew it. The rest of us knew it.

Esther, now knee deep in the surf beside me, calmly cau-tioned, "I don't think you will be able to turn him if he makes it to the cut."

Dad said, "You better tighten down on the drag a little and bring him across the slough."

I knew they both were right, but I also knew the under-matched rig in my hands was operating in overload.

Slowly I tightened the drag a quarter turn. I took a step or two toward the fish to ease the immediate change in pressure.

The bass shook his head and pulled out two feet of line as he pressed hard toward the cut. Ten more yards and he would be in the rip. I held my breath and screwed the drag down a little more. I pumped the rod up and reeled down, gaining a foot of line. Steadily I was moving the fish toward the beach.

Pull up slowly.

Keep the line tight.

Wind in as the rod is lowered. I cautioned myself.

"Easy does it," Esther coached. "Be ready. He may make a last-ditch run."

I felt I had him beat. The fish now was up. His back and tail were out of the water most of the time. Ten feet to go and he would be mine.

I started on the next pull up. Suddenly he made his move. With all the remaining strength the bass could muster, he made a dash for the rip and freedom.

"Lower the rod!" Esther yelled.

"Give him line!" Dad hollered. "Let him go! Let him go!"

I was faster by a split second than Mr. Bass. I had kept the palm of my left hand over the star drag as I held the reel.

As the fish made his move, I twisted my left hand forward, loosening the drag as I did so. I followed the fish into the cold water up to my waist. All this was just enough to keep the piano-wire-tight line from parting as the fish peeled off ten feet of line. I was doggone lucky. He could go no further. The rig had held. He stayed upright, moving his huge tail back and forth, but the fight was finished. I slowly reeled in the last twenty-five feet of line, picked a good, big wave just as it curled to break on the beach, and slipped the bass up onto the glistening silver sand.

He was the most beautiful sight in the entire world. Dad reached over, stuck his whole hand under the gills, and lifted the fish out ahead of the next oncoming wave.

Seawater slid down the bronze body and dripped off the warrior's tail as Esther put the portable scales under his gill plate. I couldn't believe my eyes. Twenty-five pounds five-ounces! I lifted the fish off the scales and held him up in triumph! Dad grabbed the camera from the Scout and took my picture. I think he was more thrilled than I was.

"Let's get this old boy to the pier and on the official scale before he dries out," Esther encouraged. "I don't think I told you, but the Grand Strand Fishing Rodeo is going on. This fish is a real contender." Esther added.

We gathered up the rest of the rods, threw the stove and chairs in, and made room in the rear for my prize.

Back at the pier we rinsed the sand off the fish. A crowd began to gather to see the biggest bass of the season. It tipped the certified scale at twenty-five pounds and three ounces. A citation bass! Maybe even a Rodeo winner!

After driving back to the pier and Esther's trailer, we took photographs in the fading light, bought an extra-large cooler, and iced down my prize. We washed off the rods and transferred all our gear back into Dad's car. Esther let me use her bathroom to warm up in a hot shower and dress in some dry clothes.

As we got in the car to go back home, rain began to fall. After shaking hands with Dad, Esther came around to my window and assured me she would get the paperwork in for my citation application.

She smiled, shook my hand, and said "Great job! He's a real trophy."

It was pitch-dark by the time we hit Georgetown. The rain was steady now. The drawbridge was closed and the light traffic was moving slow but steady through town.

As the adrenaline in my system began to subside a little and I calmed down some, I looked over at my dad and said "Dad, thanks, it was a great day."

Dad started to reply as he leaned over to turn down the radio, but stopped abruptly as the newscaster said, "We interrupt this program to bring you breaking news. According to White House sources, Soviet Ambassador Anatoly Dobrynin has just completed a call to President Kennedy. Premier Khrushchev has announced that he will dismantle the installation of missiles and return them to the Soviet Union, expressing his trust that the United States would not invade Cuba."

Our country's quick demonstration of might and determination had worked. There would be no war today.

Dad paused a moment, gave a sigh of relief, and leaned back in his seat.

As the lights of an oncoming car lit up the smile on his face, he turned to me and said, "Yes, this is the best day ever."

NOTE: Three months later in mid-January I received in the mail my First Place Certificate of Award from the Grand Strand Fishing Rodeo.

You Got My Attention

The cold salt water was up to our calves. It was rising slowly, but rising nonetheless. Both Dad and I had on chest waders and neither of us would have given the height of the rising water a second thought, except for the fact that, where we were standing, the water level for a half a mile in every direction was neck deep.

To be exact, the two of us were shoulder to shoulder in a curtain blind behind the Outer Banks of North Carolina, in the middle of Croatan Sound. Hunting from such a strange contraption was quite new to both of us.

The delicious mixture of danger, the adventure of the unknown, and the anticipation of my first goose hunt had me shivering.

We waited in the dusky purple of false dawn. The scaup, ring-necks, and other diving ducks would fly at dawn. The big Canadian geese, our main quarry, would lift off their roost and move to feeding grounds thirty to forty minutes after good light.

Waiting is always part of the hunting game. Mesmerized by the slow, repetitive flash of the nearby Bodie Island lighthouse, I began thinking about how Dad and I had arrived at this isolated spot. We were looking out at eye level over choppy cold seawater, with land no closer than a three-quarter-mile boat ride.

157

My dad was the best! He was always searching for hunting or fishing spots where neither he nor I had ever been. Every chance we got we were off to places with names like Swanquarter, Manteo, Cape Hatteras, Buxton, Ocracoke, Portsmouth Island, Bull Bay, Hemingway, or Mattamuskeet. Those spots and others lured us to new adventures. Of course when I was younger that meant I had to miss school, and he had to take a vacation from his job at the glass plant. Thanksgiving, the week after Christmas, and summer vacations were holiday dates etched in my mind for months in advance.

This Thanksgiving trip was the result of a glowing recommendation from my mother's first cousin, Ambrose Easterby. Am Junior, as everyone called him, was legendary for embellishing the details of his numerous hunting and fishing trips.

Am's description of his goose hunting trip to George Mann's hunting lodge behind Bodie Island in the fall of 1969 was no exception. To hear Am Junior tell it: "The weather was perfect. Yes, the cold, cloudy, and windy day was just what the doctor ordered for goose hunting."

"Hunting was terrific; never seen so many geese in my life. Shot more than any other person at the camp all season."

"Food – Oh! Oh! It was just out of this world. Best fresh oysters and crab I've eaten anywhere, ever."

Though normally taken with a grain of salt, Am Junior stories were all loved and eagerly anticipated at any Easterby family gathering.

Typical exaggerations factored in, my dad thought it sounded like a potential adventure and he began to correspond with George Mann, owner of this unique hunting lodge. The location would require a twelve- to fourteen-hour drive, but we had never been to the Outer Banks before. So we decided to make it a combination hunting and fishing trip. Dates were set, and I began to count the days until the coming November.

Most highly anticipated dates arrive at a snail's pace, but they do finally arrive, just as this adventure did.

A week before the departure date, Dad and I began to lay out our gear in the living room. It was the part of the house we used least. With mom's reluctant agreement, we quickly began to clutter the floor.

African safaris I had eagerly read about may have required more thought, investment in time, and anxiety over clothing selection, but I doubted it.

The night before departure the floor was littered with guns, rods and reels, shells, insulated underwear, hunting britches, coats of several different weights, rain suits, three or four hats and caps apiece, flashlights, spare batteries, a Kodak camera, extra rolls of Kodacolor film, L.L. Bean gum sole boots, chest waders, a wader repair kit, our toilet kits, and a large bottle of Pepto-Bismol.

Of course all the gear would not fit into the two canvas Navy duffel bags my Dad had arrived home from World War II with, so instead of making really hard choices, we broke our own rule of one bag a person and pressed into service an additional olive-green duffel I had used at two Boy Scout National Jamborees.

We were ready!

The next morning we loaded the gun cases, rods, and duffle bags into the family four-door sedan. We were off at 4:00 A.M.

The fourteen-hour car trip to Bodie Island would prove to be an adventure in its own right. The trip required two ferry crossings and took careful planning. We needed reservations for both from the North Carolina Department of Transportation. The arrangements were specific not only as to day, but also time.

A spot on these ferries could be quite difficult to come by in the popular fall season.

The departures from the little community of Atlantic to Ocracoke Island would be based on the two-hour crossing and varied, depending on the barrier island's fickle weather. We had to be at this first ferry landing by 1:00 P.M. sharp.

When daylight finally came we were just entering the sprawling farming country of the eastern Carolinas. The land flattened out. The cultivated fields which had long been harvested were three to four times larger than any at home. It was a farmer's dream and stunningly beautiful country.

We pressed on northeast. We drove through Lumberton, Fayetteville, Clinton, and Jacksonville. Our goal was the Sanitary Fishmarket Restaurant in Morehead City. By 11 A.M. we were starved and ready for a break. The big, thick, white bowls of steaming oyster stew and baskets of slightly sweet hush puppies have no equal. As we ate we watched through the restaurant's waterfront plate glass windows the bay's bustling boat traffic on this clear, cool morning. The new smells, sights, and unrivaled fresh seafood crowded out conversation. Too many hushpuppies and our impending ferry schedule caused us to skip dessert.

At Morehead City we left the farmland behind. The small road leading out of town wound through vast, sienna salt marshes, and winding tidal creeks passing tiny fishing communities perched on scarce plots of high ground.

There was noticeable relief in my Dad's face as we pulled into the ferry queue with thirty minutes to spare.

We spent the short waiting time exploring the clean, white sandy beach surrounding the ferry landing. It felt like early fall. The light breeze off the cool water of the bay made for light sweater weather, but the sun was warm on our faces. It felt good to be alive.

We were the fourth of the eighteen cars and pickup trucks lined up to drive on. As soon as we had followed the loadmaster's parking instructions, Dad and I headed up to the tiny second deck.

Ten minutes into our two-hour crossing Dad was fast asleep. He was tired from the early start and long drive, but I was as excited as a new colt on a spring day.

There were waterfowl of all kinds on the water and in the air.

Sea ducks were rafted up on the vast expanses of the bay. The ferry's steady progress across disrupted their nap as they flew in long, low lines to a less busy spot. A flight of cormorants caused me to briefly think I was sighting my first flock of Canadian geese or perhaps some snows.

From reading articles about goose hunting, I knew if the wind was blowing hard and the weather was cold and rough, the geese would trade back and forth all day from ocean to soundside.

But a bluebird day was the best description for the picture-perfect weather we were enjoying this afternoon. The legendary winter population of geese would be quite content to snooze on the smooth Atlantic until the dinner bell. Then they would return by the thousands to Pea Island, a national waterfowl refuge.

Due to the unusually warm, calm weather, I would have to wait until near dark to witness this spectacle firsthand.

A few minutes before docking I woke Dad, and we were in the car, engine running, when the big black ramp on the opposite end of the ferry was lowered. We disembarked and circled the miniature harbor, passing through the picturesque fishing village of Ocrakoke. Then it was on across the entire length of the island to the Hatteras Ferry.

The remote, thin barrier island was some of the most unique and scenic country I had ever traveled. Beautiful sea oat-covered sand dunes defined the right-hand side of the road. The sun-sparkling salt water of Pamlico Sound stretched as far as my eyes could see to the left and ahead.

I would have given almost anything if we had time to stop the car at the government provided turnouts. I wanted to climb one of those tall, steep dunes to see what lay on the other side. But we raced on. Time, tide, and the ferry would wait for no man.

We repeated the efficient loading and unloading procedure at the north end of Ocrakoke Island.

Sixty short minutes later our drive continued north through Hatteras, Frisco, Buxton, Avon, and Rodanthe. With every mile my excitement grew. The setting sun and high cirrus clouds were preparing to put on a light show at sunset. It wouldn't be long now.

I was the first to spot the Bodie Island beacon as its protective flashes were beginning to compete with the rapidly sinking sun.

Dad began to read aloud the directions as he balanced his handwritten notes over the steering wheel.

Follow small dirt road out the back of the Bodie Island paved parking lot. Drive to water's edge. Flash headlights. Do not honk. Boat will come pick you up.

On the first drive-through of the completely empty parking lot we missed the obscure entrance shaded by myrtle bushes. But we cautiously eased in on the second pass.

After winding through a couple hundred yards of windswept dwarf live oaks, out we popped onto a small, sandy landing. Someone long ago had hacked out of the foliage enough room for two vehicles. The landing was covered with bushels of broken, bleached oyster shells.

We were facing into the sound. A quarter-mile in front of us was our destination, a tiny white lodge set on low pilings. It was anchored on one end by the smallest island I had ever seen. The island was half the size of the building that nearly covered it.

Dad looked at me and said, "Guess this is us." He flashed the headlights several times, and we both got out of the car.

It felt great to stretch. The fading rays of the sun were setting the western sky ablaze. The temperature was warm with just a little light breeze off the ocean side. Then, as if by magic, the geese appeared. Within minutes it was as if every goose in the world was headed to the same place at the same moment, line after line, V-formation, ad infinitum, flying in from the bay to the marsh. The second they passed over the lighthouse, they locked their wings and began their graceful glide to the refuge some distance inland.

The spectacle was more than I bargained for. If I never uncased my gun, the trip was already a success. The picture of those grand visitors from so far north sailing into the yellow, blue, and crimson sunset will be stored in my memory bank forever.

Only the approaching sound of a smooth-running Johnson outboard nearing the landing made me turn away. The long, low, wooden workboat had the eye-appealing lines typical of an Outer Banks handbuilt craft.

At a precisely practiced distance from the sandy shore, the sole occupant cut the motor and tilted the engine out of the water. The boat coasted to a complete stop, just as the curved bow touched the sand.

A big man in chest waders and a faded blue short-sleeved shirt slid over the side and pulled the boat another three feet up onto the small beach.

"I guess you're the Farises? Name's George, George Mann."

As Dad took the man's hand, Dad said "That's us. I'm John Faris, and this is Johnny, Jr."

"Welcome! Throw your gear in the boat and then pull your car into one of the parking spots. Tide's coming up. It'll be quite high for the next couple days, better park in the second spot, it's above the high-water mark."

The waterfowl numbers kept growing. I was having a hard time helping load the boat for watching the heavenly parade. It was getting dark. The army of birds was still visible against the sky, but as soon as they dropped below the tree line on the opposite shore only the raucous gabbing told you they were still filling the marsh.

"Ever been goose hunting before?" George asked me as he effortlessly threw one of our heavy duffels into the boat. I'm sure he already knew the answer as he observed my wide-eyed wonder at the scene unfolding all around me.

"No, sir," I replied. "This is my first time, but I've hunted ducks before," I offered.

George looked at the sky and said, "Well, you ought to see a few of both tomorrow. It's really warm, though. Unusually so."

George instructed, "Johnny, Jr., you jump up front, Dad you take the middle seat, and I'll push us out."

The boat approached the little lodge. I could see it was constructed on sturdy pilings. The building and dock projected half over the water. The rest almost completely covered the very small piece of the island.

Later that evening over delicious wild duck and brown rice, George would explain that the island was actually part of a much bigger tract of land deeded to his family many generations earlier by King George II of England.

George deftly slid the boat up to the long, sturdy dock, and we began to unload our gear. I was secretly encouraged to see ducks and Canadian geese, shot that morning, aging on nails driven into the outside walls of the lodge.

Handmade canvas-covered Canada goose decoys and wooden crab traps were stacked on every available inch of the dock and the lodge's deck. The setting was the stuff a young hunter's dreams are made of.

As we entered the warm glow of heart pine flooring and aged cypress siding, we were introduced to Simon. Simon, as it turned out, was at the top of his peer group, traditionally known as camp cooks. His smiling face was blacker than coal, and it was glistening from the heat of the stove. Around his neck he wore a white towel. At least one hand was perpetually wiping the perspiration from his shaved head.

As is usual among highly regarded camp cooks, the alcohol content on his breath would be cause for concern if he were to breathe directly over an open flame. But as we would shortly learn, what Simon could do with blue crabs only one hour out of the creek and equally fresh oysters would lend extra support to the long-standing reputation of superb southern camp cuisine.

The lodge had roomy built-in wooden bunk beds and a large, open eating area. One whole side of the lodge was devoted to the kitchen.

The fresh water came from a well directly under the lodge. A small diesel generator somewhere under the deck was purring out our power.

While we finished up a delicious duck supper, George filled us in on the plan for the morning. As soon as the dishes were

washed, Simon and George boarded the boat and left us to unpack, lay out our clothes and gear for the morning, and pile into soft, clean beds.

Just before we dropped into bed, Dad and I cut out the lights and tiptoed barefoot out onto the large, damp deck. There was no competing light in this remote area. It looked as if, just for us, God had cast gold and white stars by the thousands into the sky above.

Dad, in a near whisper, said, "Johnny, you and I are very blessed people to see this."

All I could muster was, "It's unbelievable." As we felt our way back inside to our beds, I noted there was little, if any, breeze. It was very warm for late November.

We were as yet unaware of just how unusual the weather pattern was and how it was to shape this grand adventure.

We were both tired and slept hard until we heard the sound of heavy footsteps coming up to the deck from the dock below. It was all the wake-up call we needed.

By the time we had dressed, gone out on the deck to check the weather, gone back inside and taken off a layer, it was time for breakfast.

It was clear Simon had a bad hangover.

He was not his jovial, outgoing self at this 4:45 A.M. hour; however, the breakfast he prepared was very good. The hot coffee was strong enough to lift the varnish off the table.

By a quarter to five we were into our chest waders and ready to load guns and shells into the boat.

We were using a different one this morning. It was wider and longer and full of gear already. As I surveyed the situation in the weak yellow light from the kitchen window, George said to me, "Johnny, sit down on the dock edge and slide over into the front of the boat."

There was no room in the boat. There was a large, gasoline-driven pump near the rear. The entire rest of the boat was completely filled with decoys, mainly goose, but some duck decoys as well.

"George," I said "where do you want me to sit?"

His reply was, "Sit on the edge of the dock, and scoot yourself out onto the decoys, and lay down on top of them facing up. Hold on to your gun and shells."

I followed his instructions into this most unusual and very uncomfortable position. As soon as I was somewhat settled in the bow, George had Dad follow suit with his head at my feet. There we were, lying flat on our backs, clutching our guns, extra coat, and shells, looking straight up into the darkness. We were both scared to death of rolling off the mound of piled-up decoys and into the frigid water.

With George's short, single yank on the starter rope, the Johnson outboard immediately came to life. We eased away from the dock engulfed by the smell of marsh mud, damp salt air, and gasoline.

Shortly, George kicked the motor into full throttle, and we found ourselves bouncing over a slight chop at top speed. The wind caused the otherwise warm morning air to feel much cooler. Every decoy's bill seemed to be poking a hole in my back.

As I looked up at the inky-black sky racing by overhead, I thought, *If we hit a stump or oyster bed at this speed in the darkness, with all these clothes on, we will die right here and now.*

I was holding onto the port gunwale as best as I could to balance myself. The boat tilted up on its starboard side in a steep turn right, then back straight, then to port, and back straight again as our skilled guide dodged unseen obstacles.

Twenty minutes later my silent prayers for safety were answered as George cut the power and the boat drifted to a silent stop. I could not see a thing. Next I heard a loud splash and realized George was now somewhere in the water.

Knowing our guide was no longer in the boat and I could neither see nor hear him made me very concerned. Just then, George clicked on a powerful lantern. I was shocked to see him standing in knee-deep water beside a five-foot square box that was sticking no more than four inches above the water.

George said in a low voice, "Johnny, leave your gun, climb out, and help me hold the boat."

I swung my feet over the side, very glad to be off the heads, tails, and bills of the wooden birds. Still I was just a little apprehensive of slipping off the side of the boat into the unknown.

I held my weight on the gunwale as long as I could and finally dropped down into the sea. A great relief rushed over me when my feet hit solid sand. The water was about thigh high.

George, sensing my fear, said, "It's not very deep near the blind. The sand we pumped out to sink the blind makes a little mound around it. The tide will come up fast and high. Don't go far away, because it gets deeper fast. Now hold the boat while I pump the water out of the blind. Dad, you can get out now too, if you like," George said.

As Dad eased out of the boat, I could only imagine how much the jerky ride had aggravated his World War II back and neck injuries. After receiving the Purple Heart and spending months in Bethesda Hospital with a broken neck, Dad continued to suffer a lot of pain even years later. He would be a mess for days, I feared.

George hauled a stiff, two-inch rubber hose over from the boat and dropped one end into the blackness of the five-foot square near my feet. Another motor roared to life and to my amazement, the water level inside the curtain blind began to drop quickly. It took me a second to realize that as George pumped water out, the effect was a hole being created right in the middle of the vast expanse of the sound.

The continuous march of small, wind-driven waves caused seawater to slop over the low sides and spill into the blind, but the pump was powerful and the level dropped steadily. When the hole was about five feet deep, George shut off the pump. He had a few more surprises. He walked upwind outside the cone of light and quickly returned, pulling on a stout hemp rope and carrying a heavy, rusty boat anchor.

The rope was tied to a large piece of latticework fashioned of one-by-four-inch boards made into the shape of the letter U. George pulled the U around the blind and anchored it there. The latticework painted gray-green floated almost flush with the surface of the sound and immediately knocked the waves down. No more water sloshed over into the blind.

George began unloading the goose decoys. He pulled a batch into the darkness and returned for more. This he repeated until there were but a half-dozen duck and two goose decoys left. These he meticulously placed on the edges of the wooden latticework, causing it to sink about a half-inch below water level.

This done, our guide climbed down into the blind and, as Dad and I peered down at him, George revealed the last, but most amazing feature yet. The height of the blind in relation to the water level was adjustable!

It was so cleverly made. The blind was actually two separate, strong, wooden squares with no bottoms. One box just fit inside the other. The top edge of the larger outside box was connected to the bottom edge of the smaller inside box by coarse canvas cloth. The inside box could be raised and lowered with a stout rope at each corner.

No, the blind was not completely watertight, but the water dripped through the wet canvas at a very slow rate. A five-gallon galvanized bucket on a long rope floated in the bottom of the blind. George demonstrated the use of the essential bucket as he bailed the last couple inches of water out of the bottom of our new hideout.

George climbed out. We climbed in. He brought our guns and shells to us. He told us to wave a white handkerchief when we wanted him to come get us. He cut the lantern off.

He said, "Good luck," and started the outboard.

In short order, Dad and I were standing shoulder to shoulder in complete darkness. The only sound was the dripping of seawater onto our boots.

I quickly checked to see if I had brought a white handkerchief.

"Dad, can you see anything at all?" I asked.

"Not much," was the answer from the nearly invisible figure almost touching my left shoulder.

"What did you think of that ride out?" I asked.

"I can't believe we were lying on top of that heap of decoys. I had to hold on tight to keep from rolling right out of the boat," Dad replied.

"I think it was the craziest boat ride I've ever had. All I could think about was falling off into that cold water, with all these clothes on, in the pitch-black dark," I said.

"I guess the only thing worse would have been if we had been on the bottom and all the decoys on top," I joked.

We both laughed as a group of diving ducks nearly took our hats off as they passed over us on their way up to Roanoke Sound. It was still so dark we had not even bothered to load our guns yet.

"Fast as those ducks were flying, they'll be at Nags Head before I can get shells in my gun," I said. We both began stuffing high brass No. 4s in the magazines of our 12-gauge shotguns.

It was still another twenty minutes before the outline of the nearest decoys began to appear. With each passing moment, dawn came rushing in. Hundreds, if not thousands, of ducks began leaving the refuge and moving out of the sound to big, open water.

I shot a half box of shells before I got the twenty-yard lead figured out. Dad was doing a little better, but not much. By the time the low-lying barrier island to the east of us was splitting the rising fireball in half, we worked out our duck limit and were scouring the sky for our number one target, big, fat Canadian geese. The snow geese and swans were not plentiful in this area. They were off-limits, but the Canadian geese had rebounded remarkably from nearly unsustainable low levels a few years ago. The big Canadas were now legal, and neither Dad nor I had ever hunted them before. We wanted a chance at them. Today, we hoped, would be the day.

We were cautioned by George last night that of all the waterfowl, the Canadian geese would be the last and latest to move. So during the lull following the early flight, I decided to pick up the ducks. It was slack low water, and they had not drifted far.

I handed Dad my gun and managed, by standing on the bailing bucket, to scramble out.

I sat on the top edge of the blind and looked out over the sound. It was as if we were in the middle of the Atlantic Ocean. It was a very eerie feeling, and I held tight to the blind and very slowly slid my body into the water. Even though my mind told me it wasn't deep, my eyes kept saying, *"You are way, far away, from land!"* To my relief, I found solid bottom and I was standing only thigh deep.

As I released my death grip on the wooden side and stood up, I surveyed a most remarkable picture. I was in the middle of six dozen decoys. I was looking down at my dad who was standing in a five-foot hole, a hole in the middle of the water.

I leaned over so my head was the height of the decoys and surveyed the situation from that vantage point. My dad's head disappeared in the sea and raft of Judas geese. No goose or duck flying low would ever know we were there.

The sand bottom around the blind was as hard as concrete, but remembering George's warning, I eased out to the downed ducks, putting one cautious foot in front of another until I knew the water depth. When I returned to the blind I was carrying four scaup and two ring-necks by their cold, rubbery feet.

Just as I handed the ducks to Dad, we heard a tremendous commotion. It sounded like every goose on earth waking up and beginning to argue over where to have breakfast.

I slipped back into the blind, drying the salty water off my hands. Dad handed me my gun. I slid the receiver back an inch or so to be sure I was loaded up.

Momentarily the goose convention must have taken a final vote on the day's itinerary because, as one body, the geese, making a most raucous noise, lifted off in unison.

A long, dark cloud began to rise from the marsh. It was as if a curtain was being raised into the western sky. But wait, the curtain was being torn into pieces. Within seconds the pieces were fragmented yet again. Now the smaller pieces became flights of fifty, one hundred, or even more geese gaining altitude. They were all headed our way. All of them! My heart was racing. I could not imagine there being this many geese in the whole eastern flyway. I subconsciously felt in my jacket pocket to be sure there were more shells.

On the flocks came. Growing bigger and bigger. Getting closer and closer. The sky now over the sound was Tiffany blue. The snow geese were gleaming as the sun reflected off their pure white feathers. The swans, with yard-long necks and five-foot wing spans, resembled small airplanes. The beauty and wonder of all this was but a distraction. My eyes culled through this preview to the main event.

The darker breast feathers of the Canadian geese began to dominate the unfolding scene. My hands were trembling slightly. I was breathing the cool morning air rapidly through my open mouth.

"Dad, can you believe this?" I whispered. I could have hollered out my rhetorical question, and he still would not have been able to hear me. The clamor of several thousand geese now overhead and calling to each other drowned out every other sound. The spectacle approaching was more than the mind could process.

For me it was pure sensory overload.

But then, just at the last moment, right before the flocks would be in gun range, my mind's computer began to calculate the unthinkable. The weather gods were favoring our feathered friends this fair morning.

The geese, encouraged by the sparkling blue sky and unnaturally warm weather, were lifting higher and higher with every beat of their wings.

By the time the first flight of Canadian geese passed directly over the blind, I knew they were too high to shoot. We let them pass. There were plenty more. Hundreds more. All we had to do was wait.

Dad and I held our fire. The largest groups had passed. There were not so many left. *Just one low-flying group, Lord*, I silently prayed. *Just one little group.*

"I see a low group," Dad said. "Look a little left," he directed. We both hunched down a little. A much smaller group had roosted closer to our blind than the others, and they had now lifted off. As these geese approached, they showed more interest in their wooden cousins and stayed low for a better look.

As the geese approached I remembered a piece of advice from an old duck hunting guide over at Swanquarter. "When you are shooting geese and swans, remember the last birds in the group are the lowest. Each bird in the formation is flying a foot or so below the one in front. He's drafting off all the ones he is following. Your best shot is as late in the flock as you can wait."

I guess Dad had also remembered the lesson in aerodynamics because as the V-shaped wedge of nine came into range, we emptied our guns. The two last geese on the right and the two last geese on the left tumbled from the sky.

I was out of the blind almost before my two hit the water. All four were floating tummy-up. I grabbed my biggest one by his long neck. He was so big I had a hard time getting him all the way out of the water as I lifted him up to show Dad.

I picked up the two Dad had dropped and had to drag the birds in the water. All four were too heavy to carry.

Dad's wide grin mirrored what my own face must have looked like.

Once back into the blind we lined up the six ducks and four geese on the bench in the bottom of the blind. It was a beautiful sight. It was 8:05 A.M. It had all transpired in less than an hour.

Our early excitement subsided. The slight pre-dawn breeze died. The paprika sun of dawn had turned lemon yellow.

The only sound was water spilling into the blind. Alarm bells began clanging in the back of my head.

Water was spilling into the blind!

In our preoccupation with the hunt, we had forgotten the old seaman's saying, that tide and time wait for no man. The tide had turned and was rising and Croatan Sound was rapidly filling up our blind.

I handed Dad my gun, grabbed the nearly forgotten bucket floating in the now knee-deep water, and started to bail.

If I bailed very fast I could lower the water level in the blind, but lifting the five-gallon bucket filled with water up high enough to throw over the top was heavy, hard work. I soon got tired. While I rested a little, it did not take long for the water to return to an uncomfortable and rising level.

There were still five hours before the tide peaked. It was clear to us both that we were in deep trouble.

Dad handed me the guns and took over the bailing. The dead ducks and geese were now floating on the rising water, getting in the way of every dip of the bucket.

I glanced at the decoys. They had all swung into the flow of the tide. Little Vs of fast-moving water were rippling out behind each one.

"Dad, something's wrong," I said. No two people could keep this up until the tide turned.

The tide was really moving. I didn't want to say anything, but I wondered how high the tide would get here.

"Something is really wrong," I repeated.

Dad straightened up and pitched a bucket of salt water over the blind. He looked at me and said, "You're right. We're forgetting something."

Just then I noticed a half-inch rope cleated to the two-by-four which made up the corner of the blind closest to me. The other end disappeared into the rising sea water in the blind. I searched further and noticed an identical rope on each corner.

Then George's last minute instructions hit us both at the same instant. "Raise the curtain blind!"

I handed the two guns back to Dad and slowly and carefully uncleated the rope. When I got to the last wrap, the rope pulled through my hands, the corner dropped a couple of inches, and water gushed over the top of the blind. Cold sea water rose to within six inches of the top of our chest waders. If water ever got into our waders we would be way too heavy to climb out of the blind. The water outside the blind was almost over our heads now. The first touch of panic hit me.

I instantly pulled up with all my strength on the rope and with great relief saw that corner scoot back up now several inches above the other three, and more importantly, above the water level.

In rapid succession I raised the other three sides. With no large amounts of water now sloshing over the top edge, and with great effort, we were able to bail the blind dry.

Since there was little water in the floor, we could stack up the ducks and geese, and put the guns on the bench.

With the tide under control for the moment, we were able to rest a little and assess our situation.

I had been out of the blind and knew the water around it was only thigh deep before the tide turned. It did not seem possible the tide could rise enough to come over our waders if we were to get outside the blind.

I proposed, "Dad, since we don't know how high the tide is going to rise, I think we ought to get out and take our chances on the sandy bottom surrounding the blind."

Dad immediately agreed. Within minutes we realized the wisdom of our decision. The curtain was now raised much higher. In our heavy clothes and waders we found it was almost impossible to get out of the deep hole and over the top.

We struggled over at last and brought our guns out with us, but we left the ducks and geese in the bottom of the blind.

The tide now was up to our waist and still rising. We needed to signal the lodge so George would pick us up.

Dad dug around in his pockets for his white handkerchief. Finding he had left his behind, I quickly handed him mine and he began waving it in the direction of the lodge, only a speck in the distance.

From the time George had instructed us about the handkerchief, I could not imagine someone just sitting there in the lodge looking out the window all day waiting for us to use the signal. However, I could easily envision both George and Simon taking a little nap while waiting on the sports to limit out and get hungry.

Just as I had feared, nothing happened. We waited some more, and we waved the flag some more. I checked the water level, noticing the water on my dark green rubber waders had risen an inch closer to the word Duxback written across the top.

Dad and I were now both getting a little more anxious.

Water was rising quickly to a height we could not predict. Our clothes, by design, matched the surroundings almost perfectly. A white contrasting handkerchief was all we had to get the attention of our guides who were almost a mile away.

Our predicament suddenly took a turn for the worse when Dad's right hand got tired of waving the handkerchief. Just as he tried to change hands a puff of air caught the light, cotton square and it flittered down into the water five feet downwind. The tide began to carry it away and it slowly sank with the weight of the water it was absorbing.

I scrambled after it and got within an arm's length. Remembering George's warning about the drop-off in water depth, I hesitated for just a split second.

And then it was gone. The white handkerchief and our chance was gone.

Despite the warm sunshine, I shivered.

Our sole connection with the lodge disappeared downwind like a white shadow. I slowly waded back to Dad. We stood close together with our eyes glued in the direction of the lodge. We saw no movement, heard no sound. We just stood there. I do not know how long. Then it hit me.

"Where you going?" Dad asked.

"I have an idea," I replied.

I waded over to the blind and managed to reach the rope tied to the top of the curtain that kept the bailing bucket from accidentally floating away. I lifted the bucket out of the water and turned it over so the bottom was facing up.

I waded around the blind carefully until I found the highest place under the water. I pushed the rim of the bucket into the sandy bottom, twisting it back and forth several times to get it firmly into position with the bottom of the bucket facing up. It was a good two feet under the water.

"Dad, I need you to come close. Shift both guns to one arm and help steady me. I need to hold on to your shoulder."

I glanced over my shoulder to be sure the lodge was straight behind me.

"Dad, you face the lodge and keep an eye out for George." Little did we know that George was out on the deck in the warm sunshine. Three empty, longneck Blue Ribbon beer bottles rested behind his chair, feet propped up on the railing, leaning back against the warm wall, cap tilted down over his eyes. George was dead asleep.

Using Dad's right shoulder for support, I climbed up on the bucket. Now only knee-deep in the water, I thought I could manage what I needed to do. Carefully maintaining my balance, I unsnapped my wader suspenders.

After Simon had spent the morning cleaning and making up the bunk beds in the back part of the lodge, he passed the kitchen window, instinctively glancing toward the blind. A momentary white flash caught his eye. Simon stopped. He reached for the Coast Guard-issue binoculars on the kitchen windowsill.

"Mr. George! Mr. George!" Simon yelled as he rushed out the door. "Mr. George, wake up!" Simon started shaking George, repeating his plea, "Mr. George, you got to get up. Get up quick!"

George responded slowly and with more than a little irritation for being so suddenly roused from a sound sleep.

"What's the matter with you, Simon?" he barked. "What's your trouble, man?"

"Mr. George, come quick! Take a look. I thinks them folks in the number three blind, they wants to get picked up real bad."

"Simon, what are you jabbering about?" George asked, pushing out of his chair and slowly following Simon.

Simon grabbed the binoculars once more, took a quick look to be sure his eyes were not playing tricks on him and handed them to George who approached the window.

I had managed, with great care and assistance from Dad, to work my waders, camouflage pants, and dark green long johns below my knees.

As I balanced on the bucket I remembered my first experience at the doctor's office when he said, "Drop your drawers, and grab your ankles."

So here I was in the middle of the Croatan Sound flashing my lily-white rear end in an attempt to signal George at the lodge. Even though we knew we were in a tight spot, Dad got tickled at my unique solution and I, too, began laughing. I barely was able to keep my balance on top of the bucket.

George lifted the binoculars to his sleepy eyes and, with the aid of crystal clear, ten-power magnification, looked straight at my sunshine-lit you-know-what.

In a moment Dad said, "I hear him. I hear the boat coming!"

By the time George rushed up ten minutes later, I had managed to get myself back together.

As the boat coasted to a stop, with a straight face George asked the standard guide question, "Have any luck?"

We waded in the deep water over to the boat and as we unloaded the guns, laid them gently on the boat's seat.

Dad answered, "We did great. Got our limit, but the water's getting pretty deep. We could not get anyone's attention."

With his face breaking out into a broad smile, George said, "Mr. John, I can assure you, you got my attention!"

Just Plain Catching

I was watching George Mann expertly break big clusters of still-dripping oysters into singles. He began to shuck them as only a person with years of practice can. Then he laid the oysters on the half shell into neat rows on two broiler pans.

Dad and I had just come in from a successful and unforgettable morning of goose hunting. For the first time ever, we had gotten our limit of Canadian geese. However, the weather had turned incredibly warm with almost no wind; not ideal conditions for hunting waterfowl. Forecasters predicted more of the same for the next few days.

We still had another day of hunting booked, and the depressingly beautiful weather was lingering in the back of my mind as a second boat pulled up to the dock where I was watching George.

George introduced me to his partner, Captain Buddy Cannady. Buddy was holding a bright, just-caught, ten-pound bluefish.

"Brought lunch," Buddy said, raising the nice blue for us to admire.

He continued, "You ought to see what's happening over on the pier. I've never seen anything like it in my entire life. Fish everywhere, all up and down the beach. Big bluefish. Biggest ever caught." He held up the fish again. "This is the smallest one I could find."

Looking at the very healthy ten-pound blue, my thought was, *If this is the smallest, I hope I get to see the big ones!*

George picked up the pans of oysters, Buddy brought the fish, and we all went inside.

Simon, one of the best camp cooks we were ever blessed to meet, took possession of the fish and oysters. He looked them over with an appraising eye and said, "You folks just relax. Lunch will be ready soon. I got cold drinks, crackers, and cheese on the table. Help yourselves."

Simon cut the fillets into serving sizes. He spread soft butter over them, sprinkled salt and a twist of fresh-ground pepper, tossed in some thin slices of lemon, and into the oven they went.

As Simon stuck the fillets in, he pulled out both pans of fresh oysters. They were each sizzling in their own briny juices, curled just lightly on the edges, and golden with a smidgen of toasty-brown saltine cracker crumbs that dusted their tops.

The long irregular shells were too hot to touch, but we just burned our fingers anyway. Nothing was going to stop a half-starved hunter from wolfing those babies down. With a drop of Lea & Perrins Worcestershire Sauce and a drop of Tabasco on each oyster, they had just the right amount of fire.

As Dad, Buddy, George, and I finished inhaling two dozen of the best oysters I had ever eaten, beautiful sizzling bluefish fillets appeared on a large porcelain platter surrounded by small, red new potatoes cut in quarters and bright, green English peas. It was every man for himself.

As we finished our lunch, Buddy said, "I know you guys are lined up to surf fish for several days with Ken Lauer day after tomorrow down at Buxton, but this weather is crazy. We haven't seen warm weather at this time of year in my memory, and you're not going to kill a lot of geese in this heat. The prediction is for it to be like this for at least several more days. I know you have your fishing equipment with you. Why don't I take you over to the beach, and you can catch some really nice bluefish this afternoon? If you like what you see over there, you can call Ken from the pier and move your trip with him up to tomorrow. I'm telling you, George and I would love for you to stay, but the hunting is not going to be good in this weather. We don't want to take your money. I've never seen fishing this good. It would be a shame to miss this."

It took Dad and me about ten seconds to agree with Buddy to head over to the beach. Buddy ferried us over to our car, and we followed him to the Outer Banks pier. When we drove into the parking lot, a fellow in a 1958 International four-wheel drive pickup truck was driving off the beach. The bed of the truck was mounded up to capacity with fifteen- to twenty-pound bluefish. Some were still flopping. The local netters had been busy.

Buddy leaned out of the driver's window as he pulled off and yelled, "I'll meet you back at the lighthouse parking lot about dark."

Dad and I were trying to assemble our nine-foot surf rods as fast as possible. I kept looking at the truck full of monster blues. I was so excited I could hardly get the rod sections together. The line kept sliding back through the slick chrome ferrules.

Finally we had both rods rigged. We rushed up the steep, wide, wooden ramp into the Pier Tackle Shop. The folks behind the counter were doing a brisk business.

People of all ages and sizes were buying more line, extra lures, and bigger coolers. There were old-timers and there were folks that looked like this was their first fishing trip. It was a little crazy.

People were three deep at the counter. We finally paid our admission fee, and asked the cashier what the fish were hitting.

Without even looking at us, she pulled Able spoons off a card hanging on the wall behind her and said, "These will hold you for a little while. Be sure to put half a foot of wire leader ahead of them."

We bought some wire leader.

We finished paying, walked through the double swing doors onto a scene of total bedlam. It seemed as if every foot of space on the pier past the first breaker was occupied by a person trying to pin a wild, flopping blue down to the pier floor, hoisting one over the rail, or bent into a freshly hooked trophy.

Dad and I had caught plenty of bluefish in the inlets and surf at Pawleys Island and Litchfield Beach, most of which, by my estimate, could have easily fit into the tummies of these giants.

We each crimped on a six-inch braided-wire shock leader, added a black swivel before the twenty-pound test monofilament, and secured one of the six-inch chrome-plated, hammer-finished Able spoons. We watched for an opening at the rail and slid in. I lost Dad in the confusion, but it was clear we weren't going to get two places side by side in this frenzy.

Everyone was very polite, but dead serious. There were fish to catch – big fish.

Once in my slot, I watched a minute or two to see how the others were working these blues. I looked into the water, and I was shocked. It was as clear as gin, and hundreds of blues were chasing the schools of finger mullet. The big, toothy fish were slashing through the mass of bait. It was a killing field.

The guy on my left wore faded jeans tucked into knee-high rubber boots. The sleeves of his plaid shirt were rolled up above his elbows. He said, "Throw it far as you can. Then point your rod tip to the water to let it run as deep as possible. Biggest ones are under the bait." I noticed his boots were wedged between three blues pushing fifteen pounds each, and I considered his advice rock solid.

Checking behind me, I cast as straight over my shoulder as I could. This was as close as I had ever fished in my life. On the beach we usually stood fifty yards apart. The heavy treble-hook spoon shucked out forty yards of line. No use pitching the thing to China, I reasoned. Fish were right below the pier everywhere.

As I started a pretty fast retrieve, the lure traveled about twelve feet. Bam! I felt a powerful strike. Before I could react, he was off. I took up the slack. Bam! He hit it again. I hauled back hard. The rascal jumped immediately and threw the hook.

Within fifteen minutes I had my first big blue securely hooked and the fight was on. As I got the huge fellow right up under the pier, I realized I had no idea how to lift him the sixty feet from the water, up over the railing, and onto the safety of the pier.

While the fish was seeing how many times he could wrap the line around the barnacle-covered creosote pilings, I was looking up and down the row of fishermen on my side of the pier to see how they were handling the problem. A half-dozen folks to my right down the busy line, I saw a middle-aged lady put a four-foot round steel ring with a net stretched over it into the water. She deftly dipped the net to just below the surface. Her fishing companion slipped a nice, frisky blue right over onto the net and they pulled up their prize.

Their technique made perfect sense except without a buddy, I was in a dilemma. How could I take my fish to where the net was? Was I to leave my thrashing fighter, and go get the net? I learned a great lesson that day. People of all types are eager to lend a helping hand.

Within a couple of minutes, the lady had freed her fish and a fellow, maybe sixty years old, picked up the net and the long rope attached. He came to where I was and lowered the net next to my fish.

This total stranger, without even looking up, said to me, "See if you can slide him in."

It took three tries, but I finally netted it without losing my first trophy blue. My new best friend pulled up the net. Once safe on the silver-gray boards of the pier floor, the fellow simply returned to his own rod he had left leaning against the railing.

I shouted, "Thank you!" to the back of his forest-green Windbreaker as he disappeared into the crowd.

I shoved my fish under a cleaning table in the center of the pier, leaned my rod against the railing in an attempt to hold my spot, picked up the net, and looked for the first person I saw that had a tired fish ready to come up. I stepped up beside a teenage boy, probably just a few years younger than I was, and lowered the net. He looked over at me, his eyes asking permission.

I said, "See if you can guide him in." The young guy's fish cooperated much better than mine had. In no time at all we had hauled the heavy net and even heavier fish up and over the rail.

I left him whacking the bull blue over the head with a sawed-off baseball bat. This would calm the flopping fish down enough to retrieve the battered Able spoon.

I caught a glimpse of Dad on the opposite side of the pier with a deep arc in his rod. He was doing just fine. I smiled and went back to my spot.

Dad and I landed four trophy blues that afternoon. When we weighed them in on the pier's certified scale, we had one that weighed 14 and 3/4 pounds, a 15, a 16 and 3/4s, and a monster at 17 and 3/4s.

Dad's was the biggest.

As that near perfect fall day with warm sunshine and cool light breezes began to wind down, we counted over a hundred really big fish strewn on the pier. The ocean-bright blues gleamed in the setting sun.

As Dad and I were leaving the pier to meet Buddy, a new group of four fishermen were just arriving. As we passed, we heard the lady at the cash register telling them she had weighed in two new unofficial world record blues that afternoon.

She commented as she was handing them their change, that she had grown up in Manteo and lived here all her life, but she had never seen anything like this before.

I tapped Dad on the shoulder, "Let's call Ken Lauer first and see if we can move the fishing trip up to tomorrow." Dad said, "I'll get some quarters. You find the pay phone. I have his number in my billfold."

The call to Ken was successful, and we headed to the car with our four trophy fish. New fishermen were arriving. The word was racing up and down the barrier islands like a wind-driven prairie fire.

A man and his wife were just parking. As we passed their car, the man leaned out of the driver's side window and, gaping at our fish, asked, "How's the fishing?"

As I held up my two, I said, "Mister, I got to tell you, today it's gone from fishing to just plain catching!"

BEGINNER'S LUCK

In my experience, there is no place where beginner's luck is more the rule than the exception than with hunting and fishing.

I have experienced this personally many times, and it was certainly true of my first trip to the North Carolina Outer Banks.

By four-thirty in the afternoon of our first day on these barrier islands, Dad and I had collected our limit of ducks, our first ever Canadian geese, and we were in the sandy parking lot of the Outer Banks Pier preparing to load into our ice chest the four biggest bluefish we had ever caught. All four would be considered trophies where we come from.

Our first goose hunt was a success, but the weather favored spectacular fall fishing instead of hunting. Dad and I decided to try to change our plans for the rest of our long weekend.

After dropping several quarters into the public pay phone on the Outer Banks Pier, we reached our fishing guide, Ken Lauer, down island in the small village of Buxton, North Carolina. He had been out all day on the beach with his party of four and had just come in, he explained.

Dad's first question was the standard fisherman to fisherman, "How'd you do today?"

Leaning my ear close to the heavy, black receiver in Dad's hand, I could also hear the conversation.

"Mr. Faris, it's almost too good. I've been fishing a long time, and I've never seen anything like this. The bluefish are big, and they're here in great numbers." And Ken added "The weather is just as spectacular."

"Yes, we know." Dad said. "We spent last night and today up here near Nags Head. It's way too pretty to count on good goose hunting a second day. We were wondering if we might be able to come on down and move our fishing trip with you up by a day?"

"As it so happens, you can," Ken said. "My party caught so many jumbo blues today, they want to rest up tomorrow before their long drive home."

"That sounds perfect. We'll pack up and head down tonight. What time and where should we meet in the morning?" Dad asked.

"Let's see, the tide was about right at eight this morning, so it's no use to start before nine. Why don't we meet at my house at eight-thirty? You folks grab some breakfast, and let's meet here. We'll do lunch on the beach if you like. I'll have everything you need. Just bring your rods and raingear. You never know about our weather." Ken suggested.

After directions to his house, we called the girls, Mom and Claudia, my wife of only five months. Dad told them the change in plans. The afternoon before, we had settled them into the Cape Pine Motel in Buxton so they could explore the beach and lower Outer Banks area while we were hunting further up the island. They were excited to hear we were coming back early.

We were packed up and on the road headed south down the Outer Banks by five o'clock. We were entertained by flight after flight of ducks, geese, brant, and swans all headed to roost on

Pamlico Sound in the protection of Pea Island National Wildlife Refuge.

Dad and I arrived at Buxton after dark. We were tired from getting up so early, but we were running pretty strong on the adrenaline from an exciting, action-packed day.

We were starved. After checking into our second room, we collected both our wives, got a recommendation on dinner from the friendly motel owner, and headed over to the Captain's Table Restaurant.

The place was packed. The only thing better than the house specialty, broiled baby flounder stuffed with crab meat, was the crowd. Almost to a person the entire place, including the waitress, were dyed-in-the-wool surf fishermen. It had been a record setting day the entire length of these barrier islands. Every man, woman, boy, or girl who fished that day had a story to tell.

There were some seriously happy folks in that place, and the enthusiasm, laughter, and camaraderie were contagious. After supper we drove a short distance to the lee of the island, found the charter boat dock, a cleaning table with running water, and filleted our four bluefish.

We had some nice pictures taken on the pier to show the folks back home and now some beautiful fillets for the broiler. What a great day!

By eight o'clock the next morning the four of us had rounded up some warm honey buns and strong, freshly brewed coffee. Having breakfast together on two comfortable benches under the tall, shady pines with a nice beach breeze was very inviting. But there was the adventure of a new day, a fresh section of Cape Hatteras National Seashore to explore, and, with any luck, fish to catch, we hoped.

We drove into Ken Lauer's front yard at eight-thirty sharp. Wind-twisted live oaks with long beards of gray moss formed a shady canopy over his quiet home.

Ken was a full-time surf fishing guide who had come highly recommended. He had been a medical corpsman in the Navy. When he got out, he and his wife, Libby, also a fishing guide, had moved to Buxton and set up their guiding business. Ken met us at the door and after introductions all around, we loaded our fishing gear into the back of his Jeep. We put our rods in the custom, built-in, aluminum rod holder mounted to the front bumper. We all piled in.

Our first stop a short distance up the road was the Red Drum Tackle Shop. The place was humming. There was hardly any place to park. Men in chest waders were pumping gas, loading ice, buying fresh bait, putting new line on big open-face reels, and filling coolers with soft drinks and beer. There was an electricity of excitement that was almost palpable.

The morning tide would be best in about an hour and a half, and no one wanted to be late. Yesterday's successes and continuing spectacular weather had set the stage for near pandemonium. Eternal optimism reigned.

Ken being a true professional had avoided all this rush by getting everything ready the night before for our day of fishing. He told us what he had packed for lunch, offered to add anything by way of food or drink that we especially wanted, told Bob the owner of the tackle shop what channel on the citizens band radio he would be monitoring that morning, and we were off.

I was very impressed with Ken's four-wheel drive Jeep. When we first began loading our equipment into it earlier, I noticed not one, but two spare tires in a custom rack on top, a full-size shovel, a five-gallon jerry can of gasoline, and a long, sturdy-looking, logging chain. When we crossed over the first sand dunes, I realized we would probably need it all.

We drove north on North Carolina State Route 12 toward Avon. We turned right toward the beach, up a steep, wooden ramp. The ramp was as wide as a two-lane road and was provided by the National Park Service to protect the dunes from the heavy four-wheel drive beach traffic of thousands of fishermen who flocked to this fishing mecca each spring and fall. We topped Ramp 18. Knowing this was our first surf fishing trip on the Banks, Ken paused at the top so we could get the full impact of raw beauty that stretched for miles in both directions. In that fall of 1970, from that vantage point, I could see there was not a single man-made structure in sight as far as the eye could see.

My thought was, *What a national treasure!*

In both directions the two-story sand dunes blanketed with green and gold sea oats formed the inner border. A crystal clear jade surf defined the outer edge, and a shimmering sun-drenched white sandy beach completed this tricolor ribbon that stretched into infinity.

It was pure sensory overload. I did not want to leave this. I just wanted to get out of the Jeep, climb the last twenty feet to the top of the dunes, and sit down. I wanted to see if it was possible to soak up enough of what lay before me so that my mind's reservoir would never run dry of the image.

I was pulled back to reality when I heard Ken call urgently, "I see birds working up the beach, let's go."

As we pulled off the ramp the next thing that struck me was the amount of wood that lay everywhere. After many trips to the Outer Banks since that first adventure, I have never seen anything even remotely like the amount of wreckage on the beach I saw on that day. There were wooden beams and boards everywhere.

Long ones, short ones, most full of nails sticking out. The sight gave new meaning to the title, Graveyard of the Atlantic.

It was obvious that even in these modern times, the lighthouse at Hatteras was not enough to keep some ships from foundering off the treacherous shoals.

Ken stopped at the foot of the ramp and got out. I got out of the backseat to see if he needed help. He showed me how to let the air in the tires down to 18 pounds. This, he explained, would allow us to ride over the soft sand and not sink down as quickly. While we were doing this, I asked him about the two tires and extra gear on the top rack, and he said since the cargo shipwreck three months earlier, it was not uncommon to have to change tires a couple times a day. He said under the sand was just about as much wood with the nails sticking out as you could see protruding above.

With the tires looking almost flat, we carefully picked our way toward the birds. When we got close, we found a lone fisherman. He was knee-deep in the surf, casting through a very large group of frantically feeding gulls right outside the second breaking wave. Ken slowed, and we watched the man make a couple more casts. He did not get a strike while we watched.

We were all obviously looking and listening to the CB radio, for a report of the monster blues everyone had caught so easily the day before. Ken watched the birds closely for a few more minutes.

He said "I think those birds are working over bonito. See how fast the fish are moving under the birds? Blues don't move that fast. I think we need to drive on down the beach. There are some good sloughs a little further down where we caught most of our fish yesterday."

Dad was sitting up front. Mom, Claudia, and I were packed like sardines in the backseat. I was on the outside next to the window that faced the ocean.

The consistently large surf, indicative of these barrier islands, had cut the beach so severely that the Jeep was sitting above a two-foot sheer drop-off to where the tide had last risen to its highest level. Ken, being on the driver's side, could not see over the passenger's side window and down onto the hard, wet sand below this shelf at the high watermark.

But I could. As the Jeep slowly began to ease forward, movement directly below my open window caught my attention. When I looked down, lying not five feet away, were two striped bass fresh out of the surf. One was still flopping. Its chrome and black sides flashed in the hard glare of the early morning sun. Both fish would top thirty pounds.

"Ken," I said, "I don't know whether these are bonito or not, lying here on the beach, but I think I'd like to try catching a couple before we leave."

"Where do you see any fish?" Ken inquired.

"Right below this shelf on my side. There are two of them – big ones, fresh caught."

Ken backed up twenty yards, put the Jeep in park, and came running around to where I was now standing and pointing at the fish. One quick look and Ken said, "Okay, everybody out. There's some nice striped bass schooled up here. John, you and your Dad get your rods out. Cast as far as you can. The fish are pretty far out."

Ken was a field tester for many of the familiar names in fishing tackle. He grabbed his custom-built eleven-and-a-half-foot surf rod which already had a big, long, Able spoon attached. He waded to about thigh deep down the very steep beach and into booming surf.

As I was getting my rod out of the rack, I watched Ken make his first cast. I did not know you could throw a spoon that far. I would learn later that Ken was also a Champion Distance Caster in big-name competitions.

Anyway, the distance was impressive and right in the middle of the working birds. Within seconds he had a really good fish on. Ken waded back and motioned for Claudia to come to the edge of the water. He handed the rod off to her as Dad and I started casting.

Ken quickly got a second rod out of the rack. He changed to the same type spoon that was on the first and went to Claudia, who was just holding on for dear life. He could see the fish was a little bigger than he first thought, and he loosened the drag a full turn.

He then stepped to Claudia's right and made his second cast.

Same thing. Big fish on in two turns of the reel handle. Ken handed that rod to Mom.

Dad and I had now cast several times, each without a strike. We were nowhere near as far out as Ken's gigantic cast. By now Claudia had her fish in the surf, and Ken was coaching her on how to slide the fish up the steep sand on a big, breaking wave.

Dad and I were looking over our shoulders to see what size it was. As the big wave receded and the fish lay flopping in the suds, I almost couldn't believe the size. It was a good two-and-a-half times heavier than the biggest blue we had caught the day before.

Claudia holding up her first striper with Ken's help, looked over to me for approval. It was the first fish she had ever caught in the surf. Her first striped bass ever, and the biggest fish any of us would catch on the trip! It was a real trophy.

Beginner's luck, I thought. I smiled back at my bride, and gave her a thumbs-up.

You could not begin to hear over the hundreds of screaming gulls and the booming surf. As I reeled in with no strike yet, I was determined to get my spoon to where the fish and birds working over them were. I hauled back and cast my plug as hard as I could. I forgot to throw over the bail on my Mitchell open-faced reel and almost broke my rod as the lure went about three feet and came to an abrupt halt. It was very embarrassing.

Mom's fish was getting close to the beach. Ken had already hooked up a second fish on Claudia's rod, which was bent over in a severe arc.

I had yet to get a cast to where the fish were. Dad, being much more methodical and patient with himself, was not onto a fish yet either. I got ready to cast again, and as if on cue, the fish began to move toward the beach. The birds were moving with the bait and were noticeably closer. With the tide coming up, the fish were driving the bait across the outer bar and into the deep slough.

The big stripers were working as a team herding the finger mullet into this trap. Within minutes they were right in our laps.

It was mind-boggling to watch literally thousands of big stripes churning the clear water into a froth. Small finger mullet, numbering probably into the millions, were trying to escape the feeding frenzy, and untold numbers of screaming gulls were hovering, diving, and dipping up pieces of the slaughter. The mullet were so terrified, they would, en masse, shower into the air to escape death from below, only to be caught by hungry gulls.

Ken gaffed Mom's beautiful twenty-five pounder and rushed over to me and Dad. "You should be able to reach them now. Cast as far as you can. Try not to get too excited. Let your lure get to the bottom before you start your retrieve." He yelled over the din. "The biggest ones will be under the bait."

Dad hung his first striper on the cast he was still bringing in. He set the hook and started backing slowly out of the surf with a big smile on his face. I double-checked to see that the bail was over on my reel and let go with my best cast so far.

The hammered chrome finish of the Able spoon caught the sun as it splashed beyond the first breaker. I had to force myself to let the heavy spoon sink in the fifteen-foot water of the slough. At last I felt it hit bottom, and I began my retrieve. Three fast turns, three slow, then three fast turns. Bam! He nailed it with a solid jolt. I set the hook and started trying to take up line. Not on this fellow. The fish stripped out a good fifty-feet of twenty-pound test monofilament as he unzipped the backlighted jade-green wave. All I was doing for the first few minutes was holding on.

Ken was gaffing Claudia's second fish.

Dad was about to beach his first one, and Mom had a second one on. Everyone was into fish. It was the fastest fishing I had ever experienced.

My thought, *What luck! What beginner's luck!*

As I slowly began to gain a little line and inch my way up the sand, I saw Ken jog up to the beach, stick his head through the driver's side window, grab the mike on the CB radio, and say "Bob, there are four acres of bass inside the first breakers at ramp one eight. I repeat one eight."

Ken was very busy. He got Claudia's fish off, helped Dad get his to the Jeep, and started to the water to cast again for Claudia. As my fish finally began to give a little ground, I looked to my right to see if I could get Ken's attention and motion to him to bring the gaff.

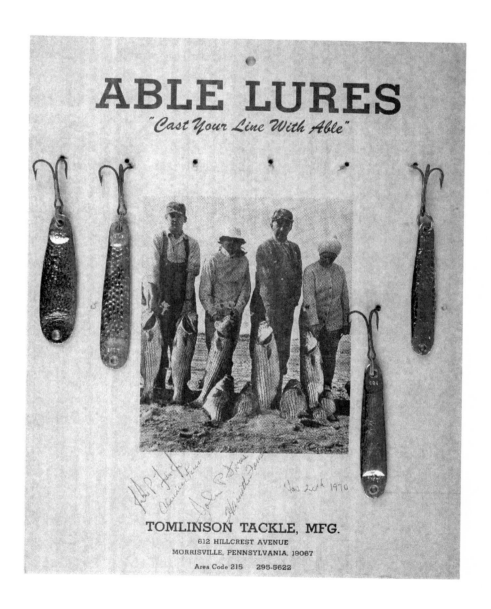

When I looked in the direction of the ramp we had crossed thirty minutes ago, there were two dozen beach buggies headed our way as fast as they dared in the cluttered wreckage. Within just a few minutes of Ken's radio call, at least fifteen fishermen were lined up on either side of us. It was nearly shoulder to shoulder. Organized chaos.

For the next forty minutes it was nonstop. Dad and I were losing some really big fish. Our rig was not quite as heavy as Ken's and it was costing us the bigger fish we would hook. There were so many big stripes in the water, we would hook a nice one and before we could get it in, another fish would hit the line and break the fish off. We were burning through spoons right and left. In between the real giants we could not turn, and those we broke off, Dad and I would hook the occasional twenty- and twenty-five-pounders and successfully land them.

Being totally new to the Outer Banks, having already seen hundreds of great blues caught the day before, and being in the middle of the bass blitz within thirty minutes of starting our second day, I thought, *This is how it must be here always. I'll just take a little break.*

I put my rod in the holder. I proceeded to get a cold Coke out of the cooler and sat down on the Jeep's tailgate. I enjoyed watching my new wife and twenty-five- to thirty total strangers haul in record-breaking fish.

Ken, almost out of breath, came up the beach with Dad's third fish and said to me, "If you want to catch any more fish you might want to get after them."

I had no idea what I was witnessing on that special day, but I always trust our guides and follow their instructions.

I left the half-empty Coke on the tailgate and went back to fishing.

Ken had called it right. He knew the fish would not stay long in the slough where we could cast to them. Within a few minutes the fish crossed back over the bar and moved offshore. Even the very best casters could not reach them. For a full twenty minutes all of us cast to the empty slough in hopes of one last strike.

And then it was over.

Between the four of us in Ken's party, we had landed ten beautiful striped bass. Latecomers to the blitz stopped by to take our picture as we lined up the fish in a row.

Ken wrote a fishing article each week for the Norfolk, Virginia newspaper and had a twelve-noon, daily, live-radio call-in-and-fishing report. He was taking pictures for a possible magazine story and the next week's newspaper column.

Of course, we four were all elated. Even though we fished for two more full days and had wonderful weather and fishing, nothing would top that early morning blitz at Ramp 18.

A week after we returned home, *The Laurens Advertiser*, our local newspaper, ran a piece about our trip. Two months later, Tomlinson Tackle Company, the manufacturer of the Able spoons we had used so successfully, sent us in the mail several dozen free spoons on display cards with our picture featured as the background on the display. We were very flattered.

But it was not until the following January when the following write-up appeared in the *Salt Water Sport Fishing & Boating in North Carolina* magazine, that I really realized how unique our experience had been.

I couldn't help but add this to the long list of times when it was just beginner's luck!

SALT WATER SPORT FISHING and BOATING IN NORTH CAROLINA

Meanwhile at Hatteras, the prospect of an impending influx of jumbo bluefish caused throngs of surfmen to turn out. The blues were to come later. But on November 20th surf guide Ken Lauer and his party found a bonanza of stripers cutting the surface of a slough near Avon, with a cloud of birds working above them. By jigging metal lures slowly along the bottom a dozen anglers landed between 20 and 30 rock in the 20 to 30-lb. class during a three-hour blitz. It was the fastest lure fishing for rock that Hatteras had ever witnessed.

After that the run was on at Hatteras, with hundreds and hundreds of stripers up to Joe Menzaco's State record 57 pounder brought through the surf on both lures and live bait. The superb fishing went on through December and into January. Unfortunately, the fine weather, high water temperatures and abundant bait supply which made it possible may never again be duplicated.

First Gun, First Shot, First Duck

At the last Stop sign on Cedar Grove Road I waited an extra thirty seconds to be certain that no traffic was following me. As I turned and accelerated slowly, I made sure the four-wheel drive never got over thirty. I did not like approaching the swamp turnoff and having to change the sound of the motor drastically, something you can hear for over a mile in the cold morning air. One hundred yards from the old steel bridge, I shifted down into second. As I made the turn onto the almost unnoticeable old logging road, I cut out the headlights. If I left them on, the harsh beams would sweep over the entire flooded area that lay below the small bluff. The full moon afforded plenty of light to navigate the narrow road.

Halfway down the steep grade the old roadbed bent sharply back under the bluff. Thick, half-grown volunteer cedars gave plenty of overhead cover to hide the newly painted vehicle from the rear and above. I had spent much time the previous summer selecting a color for the refurbished grown-up toy so that my wife would still let me park it in our driveway. Yet I did not want it to stand out when used in a natural off-road setting. Surprisingly enough, a flat metallic gray had done the trick. I was pleased that from fifty yards the fifteen-year-old four-seater wagon was hard to spot in the southern winter woods.

As we got out, I whispered to my eight-year-old son, John, to be quiet. I warned him not to slam the door, having learned long ago how far human voices and the sound of car doors slamming will travel in the woods. I was almost sure some big ducks were using this lower end of the swamp to roost.

As we eased the doors closed, a few soft quacks proved me right. I wanted those precious few newcomer mallards to feel at home until they found my acorn tree in the upper reaches of the flooded river.

Any duck hunting morning is memorable, but this one will always rank at the top. This was John's first. Oh, even though he was only eight, he had been to other blinds on other mornings, but this was his first hunting trip, the first time he had a real gun. He had owned the little shotgun for two days now. It had been my gift to him on Christmas Eve. My father had given it to me exactly thirty-two years before. It was special to me as I hoped it would now be for him. It was one of those .410-gauge over/unders by Savage Arms that had the .22-caliber rifle barrel on top. It had open rifle sights and a homemade butt plate of walnut that my dad had added when he shortened the stock for me.

Three decades before Dad had loosened the spring on the hammer so that, at eight years of age, I could pull it back. Even so, I remembered it took every ounce of my strength to cock the little gun. John was having the same problem. I knew that I would have to anticipate any shot and let him get ready before he would actually have to pull the trigger.

This morning had been in my mind for some months. After considerable debate and persuasion throughout the preceding summer, I had finally convinced my wife that I could give our son the .410 at Christmas. With permission finally granted, I began in October to scout out a suitable place for this all-important first duck hunt. By early December I had ruled out the usual places due to the hunting pressure. During the Christmas holidays I knew that every school-age boy would be combing the woods and that in the regular places only a lucky passing shot would be possible even for an experienced hunter. What I was looking for was that undiscovered small spot that would be attractive to too few ducks to draw the attention of any other hunters.

The break came in early December when I was crossing the lower Fairforest Creek bridge about daylight on the way to one of our midwinter dove hunts.

As I approached the bridge I caught a quick glimpse of five wood ducks passing over going upriver. I knew there was a large pond about a half-a-mile up that a group of city lawyers kept leased. I had watched ducks before as they crossed this bridge at high altitude, flew to the far side of the river which bent back to the left, to begin their glide. This morning, however, as soon as the ducks crossed the bridge, they immediately dropped, banked sharply to the right, and disappeared into the woods not 400 yards from the bridge. I quickly marked the spot I had last seen the ducks in the distance. A large acorn tree, taller than the rest, would help me find it again.

Tomorrow would be Sunday and I intended to find out where those ducks were feeding. After church the next day John and I were back. We parked the Jeep on a dirt road on the opposite side of the bridge to keep from drawing any attention to our investigation.

We started down to the river just beyond the bridge and followed the swamp around. As we skirted the shallow water, the land surprisingly began to rise rather rapidly. As we approached the acorn tree that I had marked, I was delighted to see that a small part of the river split off the main body. It bent back just under a rise on which several acorn trees stood. Their branches spread out over a winding creek not more than two-car-lengths-wide and knee-deep. The main flow followed the contour of the rise for fifty yards or so before breaking back toward the main river.

It was one of those spots you see pictured in high-priced, limited edition, waterfowl prints. The place was so near perfection that usually only one's imagination comes close to the painted image.

I cautioned John to be very quiet as we surveyed the spot from its lower end. We waited in the crisp sunlit December afternoon only a few minutes before the cry of a wood duck from somewhere ahead told me all I needed to know. I motioned to John to ease back along the way we had come.

From that day two weeks ago until this morning I had checked on the spot regularly. Anywhere from three to a dozen summer ducks were usually contentedly feeding on the plentiful acorns whenever I visited the little hole. I tried to slip in just before dusk on each trip, wait quietly to see how many were there, and stay just long enough to see them fly out to roost. Experience teaches hunters that, unless disturbed, you can count on ducks to return, most likely at dawn, to wherever they were feeding the night before.

I had done my checking last night. The acorns had now begun to draw a steady ten-to-fifteen ducks. The only concern I had as I eased the Jeep back onto the small blacktop last night was that someone else might have discovered this expanding little flock.

Now as we stood in the cold and listened, in near bright-as-day moonlight, I knew we were alone on this section of river.

I stooped down to help John snap the knee straps on his little hip boots. Even though they were the smallest ladies-size that I could order, they were still three pair of thick socks too big. The ground had frozen rock-hard which would make the walk ahead much easier for him. A pair of blue jeans, a gray sweatshirt covered by a hand-me-down camouflage jacket, and a pint-size camouflage duck hunter's hat that his granddad had bought for him made up his outfit.

Guns were checked to be sure they were unloaded. With shells in our pockets, we started down the road to the path I had made to the acorn ridge. The bright moon and heavy white frost made the ground look like it was covered with snow. As I crossed over the ridge and started down the gentle slope to the swamp's edge, I was troubled that the moon was right in our faces and shining like the sun.

Twenty-five yards from the water and right under the largest of the acorn trees, I had cut down one of two twin pines. I had cut the little tree partway through at about twenty-four inches above the ground. When pushed over, the tree stayed with the stump and made a natural blind.

I put John down on his knees behind the pine and let him rest the .410 barrel on top of the trunk. I had guessed about right. From this kneeling position and the gun barrel supported on the tree, he was able to sight right down on the little creek below.

I let him load the single three-inch shell. Then I pointed out to him the added problem of the big full moon shining in our faces. Again I cautioned him not to move or look up when the ducks started to fly over and circle. In the last few minutes before seven o'clock I sat with John on the frost-covered leaves for a few brief moments. I again went over what I thought the ducks would do, what to listen for as the woodies passed over and gave him that timeless bit of advice anyone who has hunted ducks gives to a beginner, "Don't pass up any decent shot."

I glanced at my watch. Five minutes to seven. I stood up, eased behind a larger pine not two feet from where John knelt, and quietly slipped three No. 6s in the Browning 12-gauge. I stood with my face directly behind the pine, broke off several branches that would be in my way if I started to shoot and whispered to John to cock the gun when he heard the first ducks pass over.

Just as the songbirds began their morning chatter, I heard a faint wood duck cry from downriver. I whispered to John to get ready as the first three ducks passed overhead, banked a hundred yards upriver, and started their high-speed, erratic flight through their treetop landing. I heard the click of the hammer being cocked as the three woodies hit the creek fifty yards upstream and not at all within sight. Five more instantly passed from right to left within easy-pass shooting range and glided to a stop at what I judged to be seventy-five- to one hundred yards equally as out of sight to our left.

I had decided long ago to pass up any opportunity this morning until John shot, so I had not even raised my gun. Now more were overhead. As I glanced out of the corner of my eye, I caught a glimpse of three in a steep, banking curve no more than fifty yards straight out over the bare willow trees that filled that part of Fairforest Creek. They completed the turn and headed straight back along the way they had come, descending rapidly. I knew this was what I had been hoping for. The ducks flared twenty-five feet off the water, making my heart stop for a split second. Then they swung equally as quickly back on course and touched down not fifteen feet from the bank. Their glide brought them so close to the water's edge that I thought for a minute they were going to walk up on the bank. This was better than I could have ever hoped.

All three were sitting motionless not twenty-five yards away, right in the middle of the little creek. Picture-perfect.

I waited, not daring to move. *Nothing, no shot.*

I knew this couldn't last long. *They were so close they could probably hear us breathing. Something was going to spook them. John was going to move, or they would see our lily-white faces in the silver morning moonlight. Why didn't he shoot?*

Just then I saw a movement from the left and shifted only my eyes in that direction. The five ducks that had been downstream came swimming merrily into the opening, now causing the others already there to relax and start their morning dipping and dabbling. My head and body were turned right. John was slightly behind me from that angle and without moving I could not see what he was doing. Before I could think of what to do, the first three ducks that had lit to the right now rode the current to join their friends. The little opening was now full of ducks. I had anticipated my son's shot so long that when the .410 fired, it sounded like a cannon and nearly scared me to death.

Nothing happened for a second. Then, just as ducks began to boil out of the little pothole, my son scrambled over the pine-top blind and waded the short, shallow distance to a single wood duck drake. He reached out and proudly picked up the prize. As he turned in the knee-deep water and held up the fat little duck for me to see, the smile he gave me was one of those mind pictures that you carry in your memory album for all time. The caption would read, "First Gun, First Shot, First Duck."

Written for John Faris, III, Christmas 2006

Come On, Big Boy, Come On!

Cecil, my dad's longtime friend and his favorite turkey guide, had a heart attack driving home late one fall morning from a striped bass fishing trip near Chase City, Virginia. He died in his pickup truck, having run off the small two-lane, tar-and-gravel, country road. Dick, Cecil's son, who had been guiding me on turkey hunts for ten years, all but quit the business after his father died.

The year was 2008 and it was the following spring, mid-morning the fourth of April. A very young John Michael, our new guide, was sitting twenty feet behind us. My dad, then ninety-three years old, and I were sitting shoulder to shoulder against a tall pine tree in the newly burnt-over pine woods. Very early every spring the landowners in the lowcountry of South Carolina would control burn their pine forests in order to kill unwanted saplings and brush. The burning also allowed the now open woods to flush with all sorts of young tender shoots and sprouts – prime turkey food.

Returning from an unsuccessful early morning hunt, the three of us spotted four two- and three-year-old gobblers while we were driving down the dirt road to John Michael's house in his Ford pickup. The four trophy birds were feeding in a freshly planted corn field not far off the road and not far from the wood

213

line. We drove past them slowly as if uninterested and continued down the road until they could not see us hidden by the planted pines. John Michael slowed and let Dad and me out. We quietly loaded our guns and grabbed our seat cushions. John Michael drove on down the road and hid the four-wheel drive truck not too far from his house. He slipped back through the woods to where we were waiting.

The tall planted pines we were hunting in were approximately twenty-five years old. They had already been thinned once. Every fourth row had been removed to allow more sunlight to the rapidly growing trees. It was in one of these wide-open rows that John Michael set up his favorite hen decoy and a new gobbler decoy that we were trying out for the first time. The gobbler decoy imitated a turkey in full strut. The *faux* bird sported a real set of tail feathers spread in a perfect half-circle fan. This pose resembled a live gobbler puffing out his chest, spreading his long, wide tail feathers into a large fan, and popping his strong wings into the dirt – a maneuver called spitting. All this a real gobbler would perform as close as possible to the hen, as he sought her permission to breed.

Dad and I were settled in, two rows of pines off this wide row, guns resting on our left knees. Our left shoulders were facing the direction we thought the turkeys would come.

At ten-thirty in the morning the April sunshine was drenching the bright green, hand-high new growth in the wide row in front of us. This profusion of spring color was in stark contrast to the ebony of the scorched tree bark and still-smoldering pine needles of the burnt-over woods.

We three had quietly waited half an hour to let the woods settle down. Now only a welcome breeze stirred through the tall, straight, slender pines. John Michael, cupping his hand to the left side of his mouth, made a soft hen yelp on his custom-built diaphragm call. Champion caller Mark Prudhomme, another of the local guides, had made this mouth call from extremely thin layers of latex stretched to just the right tightness over a soft textile frame. The entire affair fit precisely in the roof of the caller's mouth.

The perfectly executed notes brought an immediate gobble from all four birds that were still out on the wood's edge. The anticipation such a response created was enough to cause all of us to start breathing more rapidly. The excitement evident in the big trophy birds' response ratcheted up our own level of expectation.

Our quickly formulated plan and setup was predicated on this: we expected the gang of four to enter the woods and slip through the burnt timber to our right. Their dark feathers would match the surrounding landscape perfectly, camouflaging them from our view. When they hit the wide, open row, we hoped they would spot the hen decoy resting on the ground in the breeding position, attended by a newcomer, the gobbler decoy.

If the four old jealous rulers of the roost bought the deceptive courtship, they would never tolerate a newcomer's bold attempt.

A slow fifteen minutes later the alpha male of the bachelor group let out a thunderous gobble. He was saying to the hen, "Where are you? I don't see you yet."

John Michael, on cue, answered with very credible, lovesick, lonesome "Here I am, big boy!" notes on his call.

Immediately he was answered by double and triple gobbles. Our guide would need to say no more. The excited, old, jealous rascals would be on their way shortly.

Five minutes later I caught a glimpse of the lead bird as he stepped into the sunlight, eighty yards to my right. Numbers two, three, and four were quick to follow. Their necks stretched to full height, all four motionlessly studied the intruder and the Judas hen for only a moment. With their collective minds made up, they lined up four abreast like National Football League linebackers and came lumbering down the row at full speed.

This was Dad's hunt all the way. At his age, ninety-three, it might possibly be his last. I was there just as his backup. Dad would take the first shot. If he got his bird and another shot was possible, I would try for the next closest turkey.

I noticed an extra-bright, sunlit patch of spring-green sprouting shoots about twenty yards down the row to our right.

I whispered to Dad, "When the gobblers reach that spot they will be in easy range."

The four full-grown birds were steadily approaching. They had an attitude. Necks straight out and shoulders low, they intended to whip up on this brazen upstart and show the hen who the real men in these parts were.

Dad and I were beyond excited. When a turkey hunter sees his target doing the low-shoulder run, as it is fondly referred to, he is almost assured of getting the shot. The turkey is so focused on beating up on the newcomer and enjoying the spoils of the battle, that he is paying little attention to anything else.

Things were happening very fast. I could see Dad's gun barrel shaking a little as he eased it a little more to his right. We had been holding our guns up on our left knees for a pretty long time, and even the adrenaline rush was not enough to compensate for tiring muscles.

When the turkeys hit the magic spot, John Michael clucked once loudly. All four birds skidded to a stop and pulled themselves to full height. Dad's 12-gauge pump roared in my right ear, and the turkey with the longest beard and limb-hanger spurs crumpled to the ground. The remaining three flushed nearly straight up so quickly that I didn't get a shot.

Not realizing exactly where the shot had originated, one of the remaining three turkeys lit not more than sixty yards away. John Michael began a rapid and excited come-back call, and the confused gobbler widely circled his fallen comrade. He cautiously moved through the trees, and he began to close the distance a little. As if on cue, the turkey Dad shot began to flop and carry on, beating his big wings loudly on the ground. The second bird stopped abruptly, now only fifty yards away. He thought that the gobbler dying on the ground was breeding a hen, and he just could not bear to think he was missing out. Right then the overly excited second bird tore in at breakneck speed to join the action. He caught my load of No. 6 high-powered Federals at thirty-five yards and became the second trophy taken in five minutes.

John Michael scrambled to his feet and gathered both prizes as I helped Dad up. It was all smiles, handshakes, backslaps, and picture-taking after that.

But that was turkey season a year and one week ago.

Not long after the 2008 turkey season closed at the end of April, Dad had a stroke, a pretty bad one. It left him barely able to walk. If it hadn't been for his stubborn determination, I don't think he would have ever gotten out of bed again. By the following February, however, with our thanks to a lot of physical therapy, he could stand on his own. Some of his upper-body strength had returned.

With his improvement, I had begun to dream about the possibility of getting Dad on just one more spring turkey hunt. It was clear he could not make the long trip to the Back Woods

Hunting Preserve near Hemingway. I began to put together a plan to take him to our small farm on the outskirts of Jonesville, South Carolina, close to our homes.

Without our Back Woods guide, I would have to do as Dad's guide and caller, a very poor substitute, I freely admit. Nonetheless, I really wanted to do this for my dad.

Long ago, when I was much too young to go by myself, Dad took me many times to the woods and waterways on wonderful hunting and fishing adventures. I wanted so much to take him this time, since he was too weak to go on his own. Dad was now ninety-four years old, and it was payback time.

If Dad continued to improve, didn't have another stroke, and his doctor and my mother didn't find out, we just might pull off one more hunt together. I spent the balance of February and early March plotting and planning. Dad could no longer walk more than a couple of steps, even with help. It would be impossible for him to get down on the ground to sit for a long period of time. Even if he could, I would never be able to pull him back up on his feet again.

The scheme began to come together, though, when I saw a camouflage pop-up tent for sale. It was originally designed for bow hunters to shoot deer out of.

I thought, *If a hunter could shoot an arrow through the woven mesh windows, why not a shotgun?*

Right away I ordered the tent from a hunting catalog and began to look for something for Dad to sit on while we were waiting inside the tent.

A stool would be perfect for me, but Dad would need some kind of a chair with a back. Now ninety-four, he could no longer sit long periods of time without falling asleep. I knew we would have to be patient if we were to get a chance at killing a big, old, wise turkey.

I was determined not to embarrass my dad by suggesting he take an easy shot at an immature one-year-old jake. Dad's mind was perfectly clear, and he would not want anything but a fair-chase hunting experience. As always, actually taking a trophy turkey would run a distant second place to having a quality outdoor experience together.

I was in the lawn and garden section of the local hardware store on a Saturday afternoon when I stumbled onto the next piece to the puzzle. A forest-green, lightweight, outdoor chair caught my eye. It was perfect with its high back and arms. It was nearly the right height for Dad to sit in and shoot through the windows of the camouflage tent.

I did a dry run. I set the tent up in my basement and put the chair inside. It was about three inches too high to get a clear view out of the windows. So I took my hacksaw and with the fine-tooth blade, I cut the lower four inches off of the back legs and the lower three inches from the front two legs. That way there was a little bit of natural backward slope to the way the chair sat. It was very comfortable. Now I had all we needed, except a plan to get Dad, the tent, the chair, my stool, his gun, my gun, and the two turkey decoys to where the actual turkeys were.

Walking in was out of the question. Riding in before daylight was out of the question. I would never get Dad and all the equipment set up in the dark. Riding in to the hunting site in full daylight seemed the only way, but this plan might just scare the turkeys plum out of the county.

The last week of March a plan hit me like a thunderbolt. The turkeys never seemed to pay much attention to our tractor during spring planting. We had a ninety-horsepower John Deere tractor that we used to plow the fields, sow the seeds, and harvest the crops.

Routinely the turkey and the deer, for that matter, would stand on the edge of the fields where they were feeding and watch with great curiosity as the tractor and whatever equipment it was pulling entered the field. They normally just turned and casually walked into the woods, stopped at the edge, and then watched for a while with little, if any, apparent fear.

The tractor was the answer! It had a large scoop on the front that I could load all the hunting gear into, and an enclosed cab where Dad and I could sit long enough to get into position.

The second week of turkey season rolled around. I had already killed a really nice turkey April 1 at our farm before seven-fifteen on opening morning and a second, a twenty-pounder, the following Saturday morning. I had reported these two successful hunts to my Dad. Though he was very excited for me I knew he was quite let down that he could not go, but he said nothing.

I did not want to tell him of my plan to take him until it was time. I wanted it to be a surprise, and I did not want to get his hopes up. Something might go wrong, and he would be so disappointed.

I needed a warm, clear spring day so he wouldn't get wet or cold. My mom and the doctor were going to pitch a fit as it was. If my dad got sick while hunting, there would be heck to pay.

Our chance came on Saturday afternoon, April 12. The weather was clear and hot as blazes. The heat would be a killer in the tent, but the warm day would mean the turkeys would stay in the creek bottoms where it was coolest and not feed again until very late in the day. This would allow me to get us into the field right after lunch. We would have all afternoon for things to settle down before a late feeding time – at least this was what I was hoping for.

Mom and my sister were planning on going shopping, and my dad and I, with luck, could sneak off and return before anyone interfered. The two devoted shoppers drove off right after lunch. As soon as they left, I asked Dad if he felt like slipping off and going turkey hunting. A broad smile on his face was my answer.

I got Dad dressed in his hunting clothes, into the car, and we were off by one o'clock. It took us an hour to drive to the farm and unload all our hunting paraphernalia out of the car and onto the ground in front of our rust-red barn.

I let Dad sit in the modified green lawn chair while I unlocked the barn doors, drove the big John Deere out, and hooked up the heavy twenty-four-disc harrow.

Dad had not asked a single question on the ride to the farm. Now he looked on in amazement at the tractor, harrow, and the hunting equipment on the ground. I'm sure he was wondering why in the world we needed the tractor and harrow to go turkey hunting. I pulled up to where he was sitting, lowered the hydraulic-operated front-end scoop, and shut off the big diesel engine.

I climbed down the two steep steps from the cab, sat on the grass in front of my dad, and laid out the plan. I needed him to have a pretty good idea of the strategy. It was important for us to proceed without much loud talking once we reached the field where I had observed several big turkeys feeding for the past couple of weeks.

Once I thought Dad had the overall picture, I began loading all the equipment into the big scoop. The list included one tent, one modified chair for Dad, one low stool for me, one cooler with soft drinks and sandwiches, two guns, one hen decoy, one jake decoy. I then threw in gloves, face masks, shotgun shells, bug spray, and turkey calls. And yes, a camera. I was feeling very hopeful and optimistic.

Now the next trick was to get Dad up the two steep steps and into the tractor's cab. I climbed in first and tried to pull Dad up. His legs were, by now, pretty much useless.

I came back out of the cab and got him started up. He still had good upper body strength, so I pushed from below, and he pulled on the cab's stout grab handles.

We finally made it in, and he settled into the single driver's seat. I had already decided to let him drive. He had never done this before, and it's great fun to drive a big powerful machine. The throttle on the tractor was controlled by hand, and I could work the brake from where I sat on the left arm of the seat. I showed him how the hand-operated controls worked. We went at a steady three miles per hour. It took about ten minutes to reach the five-acre field. During the entire ride Dad had a big grin on his face. I think he might have been perfectly content driving the tractor all afternoon and skipping the turkey hunt.

We topped a little rise and could see the whole field falling away before us. There stood two hens and a whopper gobbler in full strut. He was a fine specimen. His entire body shone like burnished copper in the afternoon sunlight. Dad's mind, and mine, quickly shifted into serious turkey hunting mode.

The two hens were midway in the clover field, and the gobbler was five good-sized steps away, a little to the right side of the field. They were exactly where I wanted them to be. I directed Dad to ease the tractor slowly down into the field on the opposite side from the gobbler. I would have loved to have gone straight down the middle of the field to try to split him from his little harem. I knew that would be almost impossible, so we took the more conservative route with the hope that all three would ease out of the field to the right and go to water during the heat of the day. I needed the gobbler to exit on the right side because the sun would set behind the hardwoods on that side of the field, casting long shadows much earlier in the late afternoon. As the shadow grew into the field it would be cooler there first. The turkeys would seek the shade and make our expected wait a little shorter.

The two hens broke first. As the tractor drew closer they turned toward the timber on the right side and, at a leisurely pace, fed their way out toward the west. Of course, the big male bird followed them step-for-step, never once dropping out of strut. I had Dad stop the tractor directly across the field from where the trio went into the woods. We left the engine running to cover our noise, lowered the scoop and our gear to the ground, and got out. It was not as difficult to get Dad down out of the tractor as it had been to get him in.

Using the tractor to block the turkeys' view, I set up the tent, placed the chair and stool inside, moved the rest of the gear into the tent, and settled Dad into his chair. I put the two decoys into the cab and climbed back in. I shifted the big workhorse into a higher gear and throttled up the powerful diesel engine. After lowering the harrow's twenty-four steel discs four inches into the loamy earth, I made two passes around the entire five-acre field, cutting a twelve-foot swath with each pass.

When I got in front of our tent on the second round, I stopped the tractor and jumped out. The hot afternoon air was now heavy with a wonderful fresh-turned earthy smell. I knew it would be like ringing a dinner bell to every creature in the woods. Still using the tractor to shield what I was doing, I placed the two decoys not more than twenty-four feet in front of my dad. With

Dad settled in the tent, I got back in the tractor and drove it out of the field by the same way we had come in, leaving the impression that we had finished with our work and were leaving.

After driving completely out of sight, I shut off the engine and slipped back into the woods so that I would come up behind the tent. In another ten minutes I was sitting on my stool slightly out of breath, with Dad to my right. I loaded his 12-gauge pump with a single 4x6 2 and 3/4-inch duplex magnum shell. I slipped three No. 6 high-powered Federals into my own gun, praying I would not need them. I really wanted Dad to collect this trophy.

I looked out of the window that was covered with a black mesh cloth. The tent was solid black inside. Because it was very dark inside the tent you could look through and see outside perfectly. However, the sun shining on the mesh did not allow anything to show from inside the tent, creating what is called the black box effect.

I thought our setup looked great. We settled down to wait. I checked the time. It was two-fifteen in the afternoon. We were on daylight saving time. Nothing was going to happen until around five or six o'clock, sun time. My dad snoozed, drank Cokes, ate his sandwich, peed in a paper cup, and waited in the hot tent. I snoozed, drank Cokes, ate my sandwich, peed in a paper cup, and waited in the heat, too.

At six-fifteen I raised my chin off my chest where I had been asleep for the last thirty minutes. I looked across into the growing shadows on the opposite side of the field, only to see a hen coming out of the hardwoods over a slight incline. A moment later the second hen appeared. Both began to casually feed into the lush clover that we had planted last fall. I gently woke my

Dad up and whispered for him to get his gun ready. I knew it would not be long now.

I shifted my diaphragm call out of my left cheek and into the roof of my mouth and made a soft yelp. I hardly remembered to blink as I watched the area where the two hens had emerged from the woods. Soon I saw the tip of the perfect half circle of the grown gobbler's fan appear as he climbed the same little rise. The low, angled rays of the setting sun were shining through his full fan, and it glowed like molten bronze.

As soon as he was completely in the field, I yelped once more. He picked up his head, looked hard at the hen decoy, then leaned into a double gobble. He started toward her in full strut, drifting away from the live hens. He had probably already bred both of these during the time they had been in the hardwoods. Otherwise, he would never leave them now. I began a soft clucking series, and he double-gobbled again, took a few more steps, then gobbled once more. I shifted the mouth call back into my cheek. I did not think I would need it again.

"He's coming," I whispered to Dad. "Be ready."

I was sure Dad could see through the mesh as well as I could, but I cut my eyes over toward him just to make sure. He had a big grin on his face. I knew he was locked on and ready.

"Aim right at the base of his neck. Wait 'til he crosses that last terrace above the fresh plowed ground. He'll be in good range then," I needlessly instructed.

The three-year-old gobbler picked at the clover, acting as if he had little interest in the small, seductive hen or the disrespectful, ill-mannered jake.

With every few steps he took in our direction, I could hear my dad whisper, "Come on, big boy, come on."

Forty-five yards away now, and the trophy gobbler was still coming. He took a step or two, pecked at the clover, and moved a little closer. The last terrace he had to cross was thirty yards away. I had killed birds with Dad's gun and the 4x6 duplex shells at fifty yards, but there was no way Dad could make this shot now, even at forty yards. As tempting as it was to try the shot, we'd have to wait. I was hardly breathing. My heart was beating so hard, I was afraid the turkey might hear it! Sweat rolled into my eyes. I could see it dripping off Dad's chin. Neither of us dared to move a muscle.

"Come on, big boy, come on," my dad kept whispering.

The old monarch was taking his own sweet time. He wasn't used to saucy little hens playing so hard to get. After all, when he puffed out his chest, snapped those long wing feathers into the dirt, spread that beautiful, full tail, and drummed his metallic black-and-brown breast feathers, he expected the hens to literally come running to him. This one was paying no apparent attention, and it was driving him a little crazy. Forty yards, now thirty-five. Then, finally, just five more yards to go, and he would be right at the terrace.

The gobbler was now turning in a complete circle, showing everything he had. He was really strutting his stuff. He tilted his fan in the hen's direction and drummed his feathers for her. Even at this distance I could clearly hear it, and it made me all the more tense. Normally by the time you can hear the turkey drumming, he is in easy killing distance. As the gobbler turned all the way back around and faced the little decoy and us, I heard Dad click off the gun's safety. He had been holding at the turkey's lower neck a long time, and the barrel was beginning to weave a little.

"Come on, big boy, come on. Just another step or two," my dad whispered.

As if on command, the old boy took two quick steps and hopped up on the little terrace. With my tongue I shifted the mouth call back into place. I clucked once loudly. The old boy stuck his head straight up as high as he could at the new sound.

Dad's shot caught the huge turkey high in the chest just above the gobbler's beard. It was a devastating blow. The full load of No. 6s and No. 4s picked the bird up and carried him backwards at least two feet. It was one of the best shots I had ever seen on a turkey.

I had been waiting so long that I nearly jumped out of my skin when the gun fired. As soon as I saw the turkey was hit I bolted up, picked the tent straight up in the air, and flung it over our heads. Leaving my dad sitting in his chair, I raced out to be sure the bird did not get up and run off. I needn't have worried. The old gobbler was hit so perfectly he never made another move. He never twitched a muscle.

I picked up the prize by his legs, admiring his long, curved, sharp spurs and full eleven-inch paintbrush beard, and turned to show Dad who was still sitting in his chair, gun across his lap, laughing as hard as he could.

I took off my face mask, stuffed it inside my cap, stripped off my thin, cotton, camouflage gloves, and walked over to shake my dad's hand. "Great job, Dad," I said. "One of the best shots I have ever seen. He's a beautiful trophy!"

As we shook hands, he smiled broadly and held my hand a few extra seconds in his surprisingly strong grip. When I think of that last hunt, my memories are of Dad's smiling face, firm handshake, and his whispered words, "Come on, big boy, come on!"

John Paschal Faris, my dad, had another stroke and died on May 4, 2011 at the age of ninety-five.

He was the best friend I ever had.

229

ACKNOWLEDGEMENTS

My sincere gratitude goes to the exceptional folks in my critiquing group. This book would not have happened without hours upon hours of work by Dorothy Smith, the only person on earth who can decipher my handwriting. Nor would the book exist without the untiring efforts of my editor and chief cheerleader, Clare Neely. My publisher, Kirk Neely, inspired me, coached me, and helped in so many ways. Kathy Green, my assistant editor, smoothed out many a rough spot.

Rebecca, Larry, Al, and Finn were my encouragers. I am very grateful.

My utmost thankfulness goes to my Lord for all His goodness upon me and my family.

"Ten Was The Deal," written for Ashley Faris Patterson, Christmas 2006: first published in *Outdoor Adventures In The Upcountry* and reprinted by permission of Hub City Press, Spartanburg, South Carolina 2010.

"First Gun, First Shot, First Duck," written for John Faris, III, Christmas 2006.

"Big Possums Walk Late," written for John Faris, Sr., Ninety-First Birthday, June 2006.

JOHN P. FARIS, JR.
Author

John P. Faris, Jr. is a native of Laurens, South Carolina.

John received a Bachelor of Science degree from Georgia Tech and later earned his MBA.

While serving four years in the Navy, John married Claudia Tinsley, also of Laurens. Over the years they purchased several businesses and continue to work together at Oilmen's Equipment and Corrugated Containers.

John enjoys farming and boat building, however his passion since childhood has been hunting and fishing.

He and Claudia adore exploring new places. Over the past forty-five years, in search of the next great adventure, they have visited all seven continents, over seventy countries, and circumnavigated the globe twice.

John lives with his family in Upstate South Carolina where he periodically updates his Web page at outdoorstories.com

JEFF KENNEDY
Cover Art

At an early age Jeff fell in love with trout fishing, the beauty of these fish, and the places where you find them.

When Jeff is not out on the water, he is in the studio painting and drawing.

Many of his watercolors are held by private collectors. Jeff's work has appeared in *American Angler, Fly Fusion, Duck's Unlimited* magazine and the Croatian magazine, *Sportski Ribolov.* He is also a regular guest on *Fishing Florida Radio.* His current project is a weekly collaboration with Jason Borger, where they draw flies and fish in a 30-minute timeline.

Jeff is married and has two young children.

You can visit Jeff's Web site at www.jeffkennedystudio.com.

RALPH A. MARK, JR.
Internal Illustrations

Ralph graduated from Auburn University in 1958. After graduation he freelanced as an illustrator in Birmingham, Alabama, his hometown, and in Georgia.

Ralph was hired by *Southern Living* Magazine as their illustrator where he remained for twenty-six years.

Now semiretired, Ralph continues to create monthly illustrations for *Progressive Farmer* Magazine and contract artwork for the University of Alabama. In his spare time he does oil painting.

DIANNE KUSZTOS WILSON
Cover Designer

Dianne Kusztos knew the first time she held a crayon that she was destined to be an artist. After graduating from the Ringling College of Art and Design in Sarasota, Florida, she secured a position as commercial artist with an ad agency in her hometown of Spartanburg, South Carolina, and soon became its art director.

One year later Dianne started Kusztos-Wilson Advertising and has spent the last twenty years changing with the times, utilizing her graphic design skills to promote well-respected companies such as Milliken & Company and Oilmen's Truck Tanks.

Dianne has been happily married for more than thirty years and is the proud mother of a daughter, who is also a graphic designer.

To those who come after, especially Ashley, John, Cameron, Kaleb, Joshua, Grace, and Bailey:

> Pursue life with a passion. Put everything you have into it. Never settle for less than yourself. There is too much to see and feel. One lifetime won't be enough.*

Legacy Ledgers by Mike Gaddis, 2009.

CPSIA information can be obtained at www.ICGtesting.com
Printed in the USA
LVOW13s1507241113

362618LV00003B/784/P